British History in P~~~~~~
General E~

PUBL~

Rodney Barker *Po*
C. J. Bartlett *British For*
Jeremy Black *Robert Walp*
Eighteen~
D. G. Boyce *The Irish Question ~~~~~~~~~, ~~~~–1990 (2nd edn)*
Keith M. Brown *Kingdom or Province? Scotland and the Regal Union, 1603–1715*
A. D. Carr *Medieval Wales*
Anne Curry *The Hundred Years War*
John W. Derry *British Politics in the Age of Fox, Pitt and Liverpool*
Susan Doran *England and Europe in the Sixteenth Century*
Seán Duffy *Ireland in the Middle Ages*
William Gibson *Church, State and Society, 1760–1850*
Brian Golding *Conquest and Colonisation: the Normans in Britain, 1066–1100*
S. J. Gunn *Early Tudor Government, 1485–1558*
J. Gwynfor Jones *Early Modern Wales, c.1525–1640*
Richard Harding *The Evolution of the Sailing Navy, 1509–1815*
David Harkness *Ireland in the Twentieth Century: Divided Island*
Ann Hughes *The Causes of the English Civil War (2nd edn)*
Ronald Hutton *The British Republic, 1649–1660*
Kevin Jefferys *The Labour Party since 1945*
T. A. Jenkins *Disraeli and Victorian Conservatism*
T. A. Jenkins *Sir Robert Peel*
D. M. Loades *The Mid-Tudor Crisis, 1545–1565*
John F. McCaffrey *Scotland in the Nineteenth Century*
Diarmaid MacCulloch *The Later Reformation in England, 1547–1603*
W. David McIntyre *British Decolonization, 1946–1997: When, Why and How did the British Empire Fall?*
A. P. Martinich *Thomas Hobbes*
W. M. Ormrod *Political Life in Medieval England, 1300–1450*
Ritchie Ovendale *Anglo-American Relations in the Twentieth Century*
Ian Packer *Lloyd George*
Keith Perry *British Politics and the American Revolution*
Murray G. H. Pittock *Jacobitism*
A. J. Pollard *The Wars of the Roses*
David Powell *British Politics and the Labour Question, 1868–1990*
David Powell *The Edwardian Crisis*
Richard Rex *Henry VIII and the English Reformation*
G. R. Searle *The Liberal Party: Triumph and Disintegration, 1886–1929*
Paul Seaward *The Restoration, 1660–1668*
W. M. Spellman *John Locke*
William Stafford *John Stuart Mill*
Robert Stewart *Party and Politics, 1830–1852*
Bruce Webster *Medieval Scotland*
John W. Young *Britain and European Unity, 1945–92*
Michael B. Young *Charles I*

FORTHCOMING

Walter L. Arnstein *Queen Victoria*
Ian Arthurson *Henry VII*
Toby Barnard *The Kingdom of Ireland, 1640–1740*
Eugenio Biagini *Gladstone*
Peter Catterall *The Labour Party, 1918–1945*
Gregory Claeys *The French Revolution Debate in Britain*
Pauline Croft *James I*
Eveline Cruickshanks *The Glorious Revolution*
John Davis *British Politics, 1885–1939*
David Dean *Parliament and Politics in Elizabethan and Jacobean England,
1558–1614*
Colin Eldridge *The Victorians Overseas*
Richard English *The IRA*
Alan Heesom *The Anglo-Irish Union, 1800–1922*
I. G. C. Hutchison *Scottish Politics in the Twentieth Century*
Gareth Jones *Wales, 1700–1980: Crisis of Identity*
H. S. Jones *Political Thought in Nineteenth-Century Britain*
D. E. Kennedy *The English Revolution, 1642–1649*
Carol Levin *The Reign of Elizabeth I*
Roger Mason *Kingship and Tyranny? Scotland, 1513–1603*
Hiram Morgan *Ireland in the Early Modern Periphery, 1534–1690*
R. C. Nash *English Foreign Trade and the World Economy, 1600–1800*
Robin Prior and Trevor Wilson *Britain and the Impact of World War I*
Brian Quintrell *Government and Politics in Early Stuart England*
Stephen Roberts *Governance in England and Wales, 1603–1688*
David Scott *The British Civil Wars*
John Shaw *The Political History of Eighteenth-Century Scotland*
Alan Sykes *The Radical Right in Britain*
Ann Wiekel *The Elizabethan Counter-Revolution*
Ann Williams *Kingship and Government in Pre-Conquest England*
Ian Wood *Churchill*

Please note that a sister series, *Social History in Perspective*, is now available. It covers
the key topics in social, cultural and religious history.

**British History in Perspective
Series Standing Order
ISBN 0–333–71356–7 hardcover
ISBN 0–333–69331–0 paperback**
(*outside North America only*)

You can receive future titles in this series as they are published by placing a standing
order. Please contact your bookseller or, in case of difficulty, write to us at the address
below with your name and address, the title of the series and the ISBN quoted above.

Customer Services Department, Macmillan Distribution Ltd
Houndmills, Basingstoke, Hampshire RG21 6XS, England

First published in Great Britain 1999 by

MACMILLAN PRESS LTD

Houndmills, Basingstoke, Hampshire RG21 6XS and London
Companies and representatives throughout the world

A catalogue record for this book is available from the British Library.

ISBN 0–333–56774–9 hardcover
ISBN 0–333–56775–7 paperback

First published in the United States of America 1999 by

ST. MARTIN'S PRESS, INC.,

Scholarly and Reference Division,
175 Fifth Avenue, New York, N.Y. 10010

ISBN 0–312–21706–4

Library of Congress Cataloging-in-Publication Data
Doran, Susan.
England and Europe in the sixteenth century / Susan Doran.
p.   cm.
Includes bibliographical references and index.
ISBN 0–312–21706–4 (cloth)
1. England—Civilization—16th century. 2. England—Civilization–
–European influences. 3. Great Britain—Foreign
relations—1485–1603. 4. Great Britain—Foreign relations—Europe.
5. Europe—Foreign relations—Great Britain. I. Title.
DA320.D65   1998
327.4104—dc21   98–21297
                                                                CIP

This book is printed on paper suitable for recycling and made from fully managed and
sustained forest sources. Logging, pulping and manufacturing processes are expected to
conform to the environmental regulations of the country of origin.

Printed and bound in Great Britain by
CPI Antony Rowe, Chippenham and Eastbourne

ENGLAND AND EUROPE IN THE SIXTEENTH CENTURY

SUSAN DORAN

Reader in History
St Mary's University College
University of Surrey

palgrave
macmillan

CONTENTS

l

To Joanna Coates

Acknowledgements

I would like to thank Joanna Coates, Alan Doran, Christopher Durston and Glenn Richardson for reading drafts of part or all of this book. Their comments were immensely helpful and have been incorporated in the text.

My thanks are also due to Jeremy Black and the staff at Macmillan for commissioning this volume in the series, for their toleration at its late delivery, and their help with its publication.

Susan Doran

English possessions

Habsburg dominions
Portugal added in 1580

Map 1   Western Europe in 1550

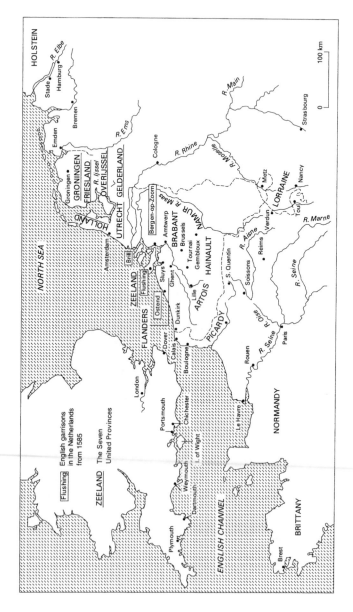

Map 2   Northern France and the Netherlands

Source: Susan Doran, *England and Europe, 1485–1603* (Longman, 1996); reproduced by kind permission of the publisher.

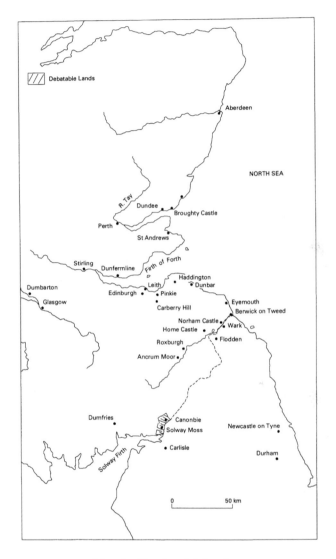

Map 3   The Scottish Borders

Source: Susan Doran, *England and Europe, 1485–1603* (Longman, 1996); reproduced by kind permission of the publisher.

Map 4   Ireland

Source: Seán Duffy, *Ireland in the Middle Ages* (Macmillan, 1997); reproduced by kind permission of the publisher.

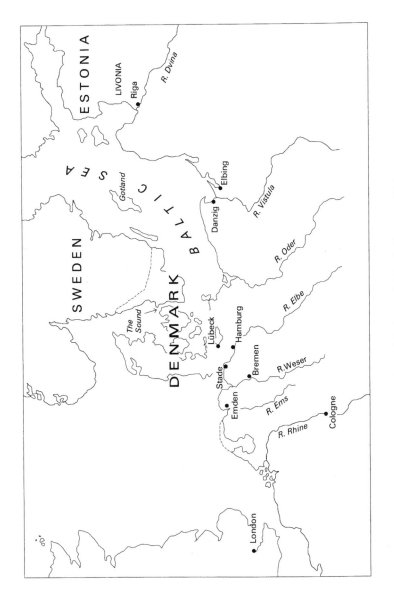

Map 5   The Baltic Sea and North German Cities

Chart 1 Sixteenth-Century European Rulers

Date	England	Spain	France	Empire	Scotland
1500	Henry VII	Ferdinand of Aragon	Louis XII	Maximilian I	James IV
1509	Henry VIII				
1513					James V (minority)
1515			Francis I		
1516		Charles			
1519				Charles V	
1542					Mary Queen of Scots (minority)
1547	Edward VI		Henry II		
1553	Mary I				
1556		Philip II			
1558	Elizabeth I			Ferdinand I	
1559			Francis II		
1560			Charles IX (minority)		
1564				Maximilian II	
1567					James VI (minority)
1574			Henry III		
1576				Rudolf II	
1589			Henry IV		
1598		Philip III			

Chart 2   The Tudor and Stewart Lines

Henry VII m. Elizabeth of York
(1485–1509)

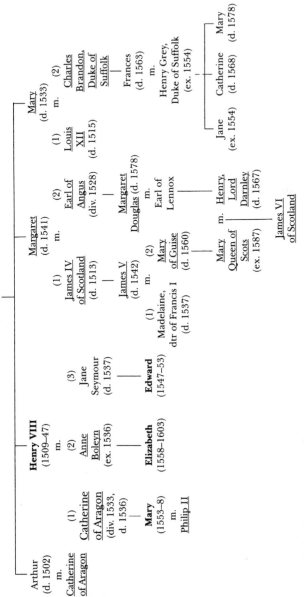

Underlined names appear in the text.

Chart 3 The York Line

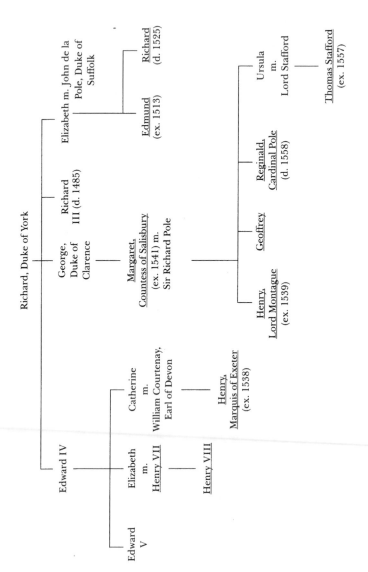

Chart 4   The House of Valois and Guise

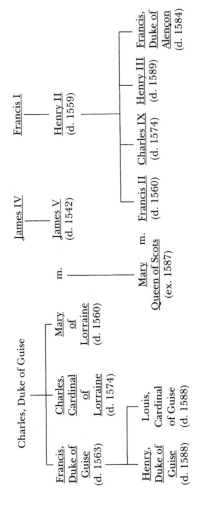

Charles, Duke of Guise

Francis, Duke of Guise (d. 1563)

Charles, Cardinal of Lorraine (d. 1574)

Mary of Lorraine (d. 1560)

Louis, Cardinal of Guise (d. 1588)

Henry, Duke of Guise (d. 1588)

Mary Queen of Scots (ex. 1587)

m.

Francis I

Henry II (d. 1559)

James IV

James V (d. 1542)

Francis II (d. 1560)

Charles IX (d. 1574)

Henry III (d. 1589)

Francis, Duke of Alençon (d. 1584)

1

INTRODUCTION

Traditionally the sixteenth century has been treated as an important watershed in English foreign policy. Historians have interpreted it as a period when monarchs left behind the medieval world of chivalric warfare for crusading or territorial ends, and turned instead towards recognizably modern foreign-policy concerns and strategies. According to this historiographical tradition, Tudor monarchs eventually came to terms with Henry VI's defeat in the Hundred Years' War, with the accompanying loss of Normandy and Gascony, and formulated policies which were in keeping with England's new geo-political position as an island (or at least the southern part of one) off the coast of Europe. The result was the evolution of a 'modern' foreign policy which had five main strands: England's growing isolation from the conflicts of the European states; the promotion of the 'Britannic idea' (the union of England, Scotland and Ireland); the development of an oceanic strategy involving overseas exploration and colonial expansion; the construction of a navy to defend England's shores and assert its commercial interests abroad; and the emergence of a balance-of-power diplomacy designed primarily to prevent the domination of mainland Europe by any one power.[1] Thanks to the successful adoption of these policies, it was said, England by the end of the sixteenth century had begun to embark on its career as a Great Power.

For many years, the detailed narrative of sixteenth-century foreign policy was analysed within this general interpretative framework. These traditional accounts tended to play down Henry VIII's later martial ambitions towards France, which might be dubbed 'medieval'. Instead, they focused on what they saw as his attempt at balance-of-power politics in the 1520s, his isolationism during the 1530s, and his preoccupation with Scotland in the 1540s. Thus, it was often claimed that Henry VIII's

1

youthful zest for war against France faded in the mid-1520s when he became obsessed with the succession question and alarmed about the growing power of Charles V in Europe. In this analysis, Wolsey sponsored the League of Cognac in 1526 as a counterweight to Charles after the spectacular imperial victory over Francis I at the Battle of Pavia, because he thought the domination of Europe by one power was inimical to England's national interests. Then after 1529, the narrative continued, Henry's quarrels with the pope caused a withdrawal from European power politics; while Francis and Charles returned to the battlefront over rival claims to Milan, Henry set about reforming his church and state under the influence of Thomas Cromwell. During the 1540s, it was argued, Henry set his sights on Scotland. His policy there – his declaration of English suzerainty over the northern kingdom, the invasion of Scotland in 1542, the 'Rough Wooing' and attempted shotgun wedding of the infant Scottish queen to his young son Edward – was described as an extension of his imperial policy in Wales and Ireland and as the fulfilment of his vision of uniting the British Isles. The Scottish policy of Lord Protector Somerset after Henry's death was seen in the same light; first the duke tried to persuade the Scots to pave the way for future union by agreeing to the marriage of their Queen Mary to Edward VI, and after that tactic failed he resolved to secure unification by conquest. The war against France at this time was thought to be of only secondary concern, an outcome of France's 'Auld Alliance' with Scotland. Elizabeth, too, was considered to have made a significant contribution to the 'Britannic idea', but in her case more successfully: 'she called out a great Reformation Party in England and Scotland at once and thus laid the foundation …of the union of England and Scotland', wrote Sir John Seeley.[2]

When commenting on Elizabeth's reign, these older narratives of foreign policy stressed England's development as a maritime power. Although historians have always viewed the queen as a pragmatist rather than a dreamer, they gave her credit for laying down the foundations of the Old British Empire by her encouragement of the voyages of Sir John Hawkins in the 1560s, Francis Drake in the 1570s, and of various 'seadogs' such as Sir Humphrey Gilbert and Sir Walter Raleigh in the 1580s and 1590s. She was praised for recognizing that sea-power was indispensable to England's new role in foreign policy – certainly for defence but also in taking offensive action against Spain. While Henry VIII was labelled the founder of the Royal Navy for his work in constructing a modern well-armed fleet under the direction of a centralized Navy Board, Elizabeth and her advisers were commended for developing

aggressive maritime policies: breaking through the commercial monopoly of the Spanish Empire, 'singeing of the Spanish king's beard' at
Cadiz, and plundering enemy shipping during the Anglo-Spanish War.
Sir John Hawkins, wrote James Williamson, was the 'creator of the fleet
that saved the country in the Spanish War and made England an oceanic
power'. For Julian Corbett, Sir Francis Drake was 'the father of the art of
warfare at sea', the first exponent of 'the root ideas of the new English
school that Nelson brought to perfection'.[3]

When England's policy towards mainland Europe was considered,
most historical surveys focused on Elizabeth's attempts before 1585 to
remain 'absolutely free from foreign entanglements'. They pointed to
her refusal to help the Scottish Calvinist factions after 1560, the Huguenots after 1563, and the Dutch rebels from the very inception of their
revolt.[4] After 1585, this isolationism was abandoned, but her entry into
Continental war was most unwilling and only carried out in order to
preserve the balance-of-power for the purpose of securing national
security. According to this approach, the Earl of Sussex's statement in
1577, 'it hath also been always good for us to have them [France and
Spain] kept in equal balance lest any of them should grow over strong'
was not a banal observation but the central axiom of royal policy.[5] It was
this principle, historians argued, that led to the diplomatic revolution of
her reign – friendship with England's ancient enemy, France, in the
1570s, and war in 1585 against its traditional friend, Spain – for in this
new alliance structure Elizabeth was responding to the fact that the two
states were not 'in equal balance'. During the second half of the century,
France was eclipsed by the power of Spain. After the death of its king,
Henry II, in 1559 France plunged into factional strife and religious unrest which left its monarchy powerless at home and abroad. The year
1562 saw the outbreak of the first in a series of civil wars which continued, albeit with brief spells of peace, until Henry IV restored monar-
chical authority and control in 1598. In 1585, when Elizabeth ordered
military action against Spain, the French monarchy was at its lowest
point, on the brink of collapse; at the same time Spain was threatening to
dominate Western Europe. Although Philip II had internal troubles of
his own, particularly a long-running rebellion in the Netherlands, Spanish power was growing dangerously in the early 1580s. Philip II an-
nexed Portugal in 1580, became the protector of the French Catholic
League in 1585, and looked set to secure a swift and total victory over
the Dutch rebels. In the words of Professor Wernham: 'The Continental
balance, upon which English foreign policy had usually been able to

rely, no longer existed. There was only one superpower, and that was Spain.'[6] According to this view, by forming a coalition against Philip II, Elizabeth was seeking to restore the balance of power and prevent the hegemony of Europe by one state. In this way she was setting the mould for future generations of English foreign-policy makers: William III who built up a coalition against Louis XIV, William Pitt against Napoleon and Winston Churchill against Hitler.

In recent years, historians have begun to question this analytical framework and narrative account. For most of them, they smack of an old-fashioned British nationalism distasteful to late-twentieth century scholarship. In addition, teleological history is now recognised as methodologically suspect. Historians today are rightly dubious about the value of looking at past events through the strait-jacket of hindsight, as it distorts our understanding of the experiences as they happened at the time. Apart from these general objections, more recent research has revealed some of the inadequacies of earlier analyses and shown that certain aspects need modification, while others require total re-thinking.

This survey, therefore, presents an alternative model and account of foreign policy in the sixteenth century. First, it does not slide over the discontinuities in foreign policy nor treat them either as 'crosscurrents' which had no significance in the evolutionary development of policy, or as natural adjustments to England's new role as an Atlantic rather than a Continental power. On the contrary, discontinuities are shown in this account to be a central characteristic of foreign policy, the result of the very nature of policy-making. As will be seen, policy-making was not the simple implementation of a clear set of principles held by monarchs and their ministers. It was generally made up of *ad hoc* responses to unanticipated events occurring both at home and abroad, whether factional politics in Scotland, internal unrest in France or whatever. Understandably therefore, monarchs tended to be opportunistic and flexible rather than completely committed to any one line of action. At the same time, their decisions were commonly taken after considerable consultation. Although Henry VIII certainly had his own views about foreign policy, he also listened to his ministers, councillors, courtiers and occasionally theologians. As political fortunes waxed and waned according to the king's whim, there were occasions when policy shifts followed changes in ministers. One historian wrote of Henry's reign that 'the pursuit of long-term policies was frequently stymied by the vagaries of court politics, which depended on the changing likes and dislikes of the monarch'.

This may well be an overstatement, as there was no major policy-change following the fall of Wolsey; none the less, the rise and fall of Thomas Cromwell resulted in some new directions in policy.[7] In Elizabeth's reign the wider views of ambassadors, merchants and agents abroad were canvassed and considered, while the council discussed at length, both formally and informally, courses of action to take in the face of some emergency. Not surprisingly, different viewpoints emerged, and it was difficult for Elizabeth to pick her way through these divergent opinions and follow a consistent path.

Second, this survey questions the modernity of sixteenth-century foreign policy. It sees continuities with the medieval past along with similarities between early-modern and late-medieval preoccupations and priorities. In addition, it gives personal competition between monarchs as much weight as geo-political factors in explaining international relations. Thus, Henry VIII is shown to be more influenced by fifteenth-century works of chivalry and examples of successful medieval kings than by Italian Renaissance writings on power politics. Building on the work of Steven Gunn, the text demonstrates that Henry's determination to prove his honour, preferably on the battlefield, and assertion of his dynastic claims to lands in France dominated his thinking both at the beginning and end of the reign.[8] His intense rivalry with Francis I is also seen to have affected diplomacy and foreign policy during periods of peace as well as war. As far as Scotland is concerned, the argument in this text follows the interpretation of David Head and others by demonstrating that the northern kingdom was always of secondary interest to Henry and that any ambitions to secure mastery of the British Isles remained a far lower priority than continental warfare throughout his reign.[9] Furthermore, the contention here is that Henry's relations with the Scottish monarchs were influenced not only by England's traditional concern about border security but also by the king's personal pursuit of reputation and honour. It will be seen that Henry looked as much to the past for inspiration in his dealings with Scotland as with France. While his model of kingship for the latter was Henry V, for the former it was Edward I, whose claim to overlordship over the northern kingdom he revived during his own attempts to hammer the Scots. For most of his reign, moreover, Henry showed little interest in uniting England and Scotland by a dynastic marriage. Before the birth of Princess Mary in 1516 he refused to recognize the Scottish king's place in the succession; afterwards he preferred his young daughter (his sole heir until 1533) to marry a French prince or Charles V rather than the King of Scotland. In his will, he ignored the rights of the Stewart line altogether and left the throne to the descendants of his younger sister Mary Tudor in the event of Elizabeth dying without issue (see Chart 2). The marriage between Mary Queen of Scots and Prince Edward was intended as a cheap way of controlling a difficult neighbour and not as the realisation of a vision to create a united Britain.

As far as Elizabeth is concerned, the case for her modernity is superficially stronger: after all, she ended the Plantagenet wars of conquest in France, followed policies of national defence, and tried to develop England's commerce. But it is contended here that in advancing these policies she was not laying down new principles (or taking up the relay baton of Henry VII, dropped by her father) but reacting to the realities of her situation in a conventional way. As will be seen, England did not have the resources to win and hold on to territory in France – even a divided France – as the abortive Newhaven expedition of 1563 proved. No monarch – medieval or early-modern, or modern come to that – could afford to neglect England's prosperity and security. Elizabeth and her ministers felt compelled to be pro-active and develop new markets because of disruption to the staple at Antwerp (the town which was the principal entrepôt for English exports) and the perceived threat from the Catholic powers. In other areas of policy, Elizabeth failed to display any vision for the future. Her assistance to the Scottish Protestants in the 1560s was not intended to promote the union of Scotland and England but to provide for her own defence; at no time, moreover, would Elizabeth facilitate the succession of James VI by naming him her heir. It will also be seen that despite the imperial propaganda in the latter decades of her reign, Elizabeth had little interest in establishing an empire, while her sea-captains were more dedicated to plundering Spanish bullion and goods than developing long-term commercial opportunities. It is also doubtful whether Elizabeth thought in terms of balance-of-power politics. Later chapters will show that the treaty with France in 1572 was designed simply to protect England from a hostile Spain and detach the French monarch permanently from the influence of the Catholic Guise faction; it had no offensive function at all. Similarly, Elizabeth's war against Spain was not 'to impeach the power' of Philip II; this rhetoric was only employed to encourage the French king to help the Dutch rebels against his traditional enemy. Elizabeth's immediate objective in 1585 was only to force Philip into signing a peace-treaty with his rebellious subjects which would leave him with sovereignty over the Netherlands but remove his military presence from the Channel. Admittedly, some of her ministers had more grandiose aims in mind, but these were related to advancing the godly cause in Europe not keeping in check the secular power of the King of Spain.

Third, this survey challenges the notion that the sixteenth century saw the birth of England as a Great Power. Throughout the text, the weaknesses of England's armed forces are stressed, together with the limiting factor of an inadequate royal income to support foreign war. Whereas in the late Middle Ages, England's military power was out of all proportion to its population or size, by the mid-1540s England was incapable of matching the military might of either France or Spain. It is true that Henry was successful in putting together some 40,000 men for the invasion of France in 1544, but the strain on the Crown's resources and the country's economy was enormous, and the exercise could not be repeated. The armies which went abroad under Mary and Elizabeth were far smaller in size and had to operate simply as reinforcements for their allies. As Elizabeth pointed out, war was 'a sieve, that spends as it receives'; provisioning, soldiers' pay, not to mention the cost of weapons, ordnance and fortifications, drained the royal purse. Financing the French and Scottish wars in England in the middle years of the century proved beyond the Crown's means and resulted in currency debasements, consequent inflation, sales of royal lands and huge debts. Nor could English monarchs always rely on their taxpayers to contribute large sums. Taxation, lay and clerical, contributed little more than a quarter of the costs of war, yet even so it was felt to be burdensome. Although by contemporary European standards England was lightly taxed, its richest inhabitants were caught by every levy and had to sell assets to meet tax demands. Not surprisingly, therefore, there were examples of objections, even resistance, to the monarch's financial impositions in the mid-1520s, during the 1540s and in the final stages of Mary's French war. It is no wonder then that Elizabeth tried to avoid war after her early expensive yet fruitless expedition to France in 1563; nor that when she did go to war after 1585, she did everything 'by halves', trying to keep the costs as low as possible. Even so, in the war years between 1598 and 1603 some 75 per cent of the state's revenues were devoted to military expenditure, and Elizabeth was forced to fall back on financial expedients such as monopolies which proved unpopular at home.[10]

What is more, the English army could not compete with its European rivals in technology and training. Only 7 per cent of Henry VIII's native troops had arquebuses (firearms) in 1544, compared to over 30 per cent of the French infantry, which was itself way behind the Spanish *tercios*

(Spanish infantry regiments). It was not until Mary's reign that the first moves to introduce the pike (the standard European infantry weapon) into general use were made. As late as 1588, England was still making use of the longbow, by then the dinosaur of continental warfare. Even in their fortifications, the English lagged behind Europe. Certainly Henry was a great builder, but he made no use of the Italian engineers who were the leading experts in the field, and it was only in 1589 that an English military theorist showed much awareness of Continental methods of fortification. Again, the training of bodies of troops was usual in mid-century Europe, a necessary response to the new weapons and techniques of the 'Military Revolution', but in England regular training did not begin until the last quarter of the century.[11]

By contrast, on the naval side, England made great advances; yet even here the achievements should not be exaggerated. The Royal Navy itself remained relatively small and English fighting fleets were heavily dependent on private shipping; the Royal Navy, for example, provided only 34 of the 197 ships mobilized to fight against the Spanish Armada in 1588. The extent of English sea-power was also limited. After all, Henry VIII's new fleet could not prevent the French from entering the Solent, and landing at Seaford and the Isle of Wight. As for the English victory over the Spanish Armada, many historians today argue that the Spanish fleet was defeated by the weather not by the superior fighting force of the English navy. At the battle on 8 August, so often acclaimed as an English triumph, the Armada survived almost unscathed; only one ship sank outright as a result of the English action while merely three others were badly disabled. Indeed the Spanish fleet sailed through the Channel virtually intact, losing only six in all of its 125 ships and only two of those through enemy action. It was the return journey via Scotland and Ireland that destroyed the Armada – a third of its ships and two-thirds of its 30,000 seamen were lost. Furthermore, although England's superiority in artillery and in the manoeuvrability of its ships is still generally acknowledged, some historians are now critical of the English effort: Felipe Fernandez-Armesto, for example, wrote of the 'ineffectiveness' of English tactics and the 'feebleness' of their close-range gunnery. Not all would agree with this judgement, but there can be no doubt that the effects of the Armada's defeat were not as momentous as previously thought. England did not thereafter enjoy mastery of the seas, and Spanish hegemony of the Atlantic was to last well into the seventeenth century, when it would be challenged by the Dutch rather than the English. Philip II had the financial resources to rebuild his fleet with better ships, and launch three more armadas between 1596 and 1599. Throughout that decade, the Spaniards successfully protected their Indies treasure-ships from English strikes and consequently received more silver from the Americas than ever before. Sir Richard Grenville was killed in an unsuccessful encounter with Spanish galleons; Sir Francis Drake and Sir John Hawkins died during an unsuccessful bid to wrest Panama from them.[12]

Fourth, this survey emphasizes a theme which is too often neglected in other works: the role of religion in the making of policy.[13] Its absence elsewhere can easily be explained. Denial of any kind of ideological motivation fitted well with the interpretation of the Tudors as rational 'modern' exponents of international diplomacy. Traditionally, all the Tudors (bar Mary I) as well as most of their leading ministers were seen as secular in their thinking. Furthermore, the traditional emphasis on England's growing isolationism after the break with Rome blinded historians to the significance of various English efforts to form a Protestant league. As a result of this approach, Thomas Cromwell's attempts to build up a pan-Protestant alliance in the 1530s were thought to be only for the sake of short-term political expediency, and to have failed because the Germans wanted an alliance based on a confessional accord which was unacceptable to Henry. The king's Reformation, it was alleged, came from political not religious concerns and his foreign policy similarly had no ideological base. It became a historical commonplace, moreover, to say that Elizabeth 'believed that territorial and dynastic considerations were of greater importance than religion in the determination of policy'.[14] For many historians, Elizabeth I belied her contemporary image as a Protestant queen. Her conservatism and dislike of rebels, they claimed, took precedence over any sympathy for European Protestants, and she gave minimal assistance to her co-religionists in Europe before 1585. At last when she did intervene in their struggles, her motives were to preserve England's national interests and not to support the godly cause. This secular approach, it was said, was shared by William Cecil (Lord Burghley after 1571) who, according to Conyers Read, his most influential biographer, 'inclined rather to discount the force of religion in Continental affairs' and 'preferred national considerations before religious ones'. As a result of their partnership, contended Read, the ideologues such as Sir Francis Walsingham were kept in check and had little or no influence on policy.[15]

This picture, however, is now being challenged and the role of religion recognized as more significant and complex. Recent archival work in Germany and Scandinavia has thrown new light on the attempts by both Henry VIII and Elizabeth I to form pan-Protestant alliances with the German states. This diplomacy can now take its proper place at the centre rather than on the periphery of English foreign policy, and as a result it has to be questioned whether England did adopt an isolationist approach to Continental affairs in the sixteenth century. This survey will show how religious considerations played an important role in the formation of policy as well as in the outcomes of the negotiations with the Germans. On a different but related note, recent work on Cecil has revealed that the contrast between him and Walsingham has been exaggerated, and that both shared an 'apocalyptic' view of contemporary politics, whereby the true gospel of the European Protestants was under threat of overthrow from the dark forces of international Catholicism.[16] As for Elizabeth, it will be argued here that she was not immune to the cries of her persecuted 'brethren' and used diplomacy and informal means of help, whenever possible, to protect them. As far as she and most Englishmen and women were concerned, it was difficult, even impossible, to separate religious and political interests.

Finally, this survey argues that the Reformation was a major influence on foreign policy. Although its impact before 1558 was more muted than afterwards, I seek to show that even then it informed many aspects of foreign policy. In the short-term, Henry VIII's early attempts to secure an annulment and his ultimate break with Rome steered diplomacy towards a pro-French rather than pro-imperial alliance between 1527 and 1540. In the longer term, England's move into first schism then heresy intensified and complicated traditional problems of security and defence. Rebellion in Ireland took on a more dangerous quality when rebels could appeal to foreign rulers on religious grounds, as when the Earl of Kildare offered the overlordship of Ireland to the pope or Charles V in place of the schismatic Henry. Likewise, the urgency of expelling foreign influence from Scotland increased when it was feared that the French might launch a Catholic crusade from the north into England. Under Edward VI the Reformation allowed the Duke of Somerset to use religious justifications for his invasion of Scotland, exhorting the Scots to repudiate Rome, reject the French and work for the union of a Protestant British Isles.

After 1558, however, the fallout from the Reformation was still greater, and this survey illustrates how the religious dimension pervaded every area of foreign policy; how the Catholic threat from abroad appeared to be an unrelenting feature of Elizabeth's reign; and how the queen's foreign policy was largely a response to it. Furthermore, it demonstrates that England could not stand aloof from the confessional strife which was endemic in Western Europe after 1560. Not only did the conflicts in France and the Netherlands directly affect the security of the realm, but English Protestants also felt a responsibility for the fate of their co-religionists abroad. It will be seen that the breakdown of relations with Spain owed very little to commercial rivalry or balance-of-power considerations, and a great deal to the fear that Philip II was the pope's deputy, dedicated to extirpating heresy not only in his own territories but throughout Europe. In France the Guises were also viewed as agents of the pope, and whenever they were in power Elizabeth's policy was directed towards helping the Huguenots. It was only possible for Elizabeth to reach a rapprochement with Charles IX in 1572, because he was then free from Guise control and proving ready to tolerate his Protestant subjects. As far as Anglo-Scottish relations were concerned, the Reformation in both realms provided the opportunity for collaboration. In Edward's reign, Protestants such as James Henrisoun urged their fellow Scots to work for 'a godly union' of England and Scotland. During Elizabeth's reign, the Protestants lords no longer looked to the French for protection, but preferred an alliance with their Protestant neighbour to the south; this provided the basis of an amity which just about survived the many political upheavals within Scotland .

The structure of this book is intended to highlight the five elements of this new approach. Within each chapter the material is organized chronologically so that the opportunistic and inconsistent nature of foreign policy can be traced: its shifts from 1525 to 1540 are followed in Chapter 4 (Parts i and ii), while Elizabeth's *ad hoc* reactions to events in Scotland and on the Continent are tracked in Chapter 3 (Parts i and iii). At the same time, the overall structure of the book is thematic – its aim being to bring out the main influences on policy. Henry's preoccupation with France, his attraction to the chivalric ideal and the importance of personal rivalry in his relationships are handled in Chapter 2 (Parts i–iii); whilst Chapter 2 (Part iv) explores the reasons behind the move away from Continental warfare for territorial gain and the pursuit of glory, the emphasis here being on England's economic and military deficiencies. The impact of the Reformation on England's old strategic problems of defence is highlighted in Chapter 3. In addition, the final section of Chapter 3 examines the nature of Elizabethan policy towards the balance of power in Europe. The theme of Chapter 4 is the role of religion in the making of foreign policy, and once again the importance of the Reformation can be appreciated. Finally, in Chapter 5 Is discuss the influence of the merchant community on the making of policy, the impulses behind the attempts to find markets within Europe, the nature and purpose of privateering, and the extent of the imperial ideal.

2

HONOUR AND REPUTATION

When in Chapter 21 of *The Prince*, Niccolò Machiavelli considered 'How a prince must act to win honour', he began with the statement, 'Nothing brings a prince more prestige than great campaigns and striking demonstrations of his personal abilities.'[1] Here, in associating honour with reputation and warlike behaviour, Machiavelli was articulating the early sixteenth-century concept of aristocratic honour and partially explaining the prevalence of war in the first half of that century. Henry VIII, however, did not take Machiavelli's *realpolitik* examination of Italian Renaissance politics as his model. Instead, his thinking about honour and reputation was influenced by late-medieval works of romance and books on chivalry, which were circulating the English court in the late fifteenth and early sixteenth centuries. In these writings honour was won through adherence to a strict code of conduct built around martial virtues, while war was represented as the opportunity and arena for the acquisition of honour. In the *Boke of St Albans,* for example, first printed in 1486, qualities of fortitude, prudence, wisdom and steadfastness, as they were displayed in battle, were described as the hallmarks of a gentleman deserving of honour. Ramón Lull's *Book of the Order of Chivalry* (translated by William Caxton) laid down a code of honour related especially to warfare, which was as binding on a prince as on any other knight. Traditional tales of chivalry, such as *Huon of Bordeaux* and *Arthur of Little Britain*, presented war as both a quest for honour and a test of valour. Although it is not known whether Henry read any of these books himself, many of them underwent many reprints and their ideas appear to have been absorbed into early-Tudor court culture. Henry VII's royal library, moreover, contained many Burgundian illuminated romances and histories which incorporated chivalric ideals.[2]

Pageantry and tournaments at the early Tudor court also did much to embed this notion of honour in the outlook of Henry and his nobility.

Recognizing that the chivalric tradition could be exploited to promote the Tudor dynasty, Henry VII had sponsored elaborate and splendid tournaments to celebrate royal events such as the marriage of his eldest son, Arthur, to Princess Catherine of Aragon in 1501. There had been at least thirteen tournaments at court during the last seven and a half years of his reign. These tournaments were not just occasions for ceremonial display; they were also seen as a preparation for warfare in the service of the king and expressed the values of a military society. Young noblemen who did consistently well in them were invited to join the military chivalric Order of the Garter, alongside Henry VII's most trusted councillors.[3] The young Prince Henry himself was encouraged by his father to participate at the tiltyard and take his place at the head of the ranks of the nobility. At the age of three he had been appointed Earl Marshall, head of the College of Arms, a tribunal which arbitrated in matters of honour and the law of arms. In 1507 he had watched jousting at court with enthusiasm. A year later he was no longer prepared to sit on the sidelines, and throughout the summer of 1508 he entered the fray, apparently beating all his opponents at the ring and jousts. Once king, he arranged and participated in tournaments to mark the most important events of his reign, at least until he fell heavily and injured himself at one in 1536.[4]

Honour, therefore, demanded that the young Henry VIII should test himself in personal warfare. He himself was 'not unmindful that it was his duty to seek fame by military skill', while others urged him on to emulate the military prowess of his namesake, Henry V, the victor at the Battle of Agincourt. But honour also dictated that any war he fought should be a just war. Military action simply to acquire new territory might have been deserving of praise in the pen of Machiavelli, but such self-interested motives were generally thought dishonourable and could hardly be advanced by a Christian prince to defend a resort to arms. The standard medieval justifications of warfare had been the protection of Christendom, resistance to unprovoked aggression, and the response to specific injuries inflicted on a prince or his subjects; and throughout his reign Henry VIII consistently used this mode of rhetoric to justify his invasions of France and Scotland.[5] As far as he was concerned, the king of France had dealt him an injury by usurping his 'lawfull enheritaunce', the ancestral lands of Normandy, Gascony, Guienne, Anjou and Maine, together with the crown of France. In 1512 royal propagandists wrote tracts which presented the war as an assertion of Henry's dynastic rights and in 1543 the declaration of war against France demanded that

Francis I yield to Henry his rightful inheritance. As justification for his war against Scotland in 1542, the king claimed he was forced into military action 'for preservacion of our honoure and right'. In his proclamation of war, he listed specific injuries which required redress, claiming that 'under a coloure of fayre speche and flatteryng wordes, we be in dedes so injured, contemped and dispised, as we ought not with sufferaunce to pretermitte and passe over'.[6] There can be little doubt that on the whole Henry VIII believed his own rhetoric. Henry's claim of over-lordship over Scotland moreover, was also entirely traditional. As Roger Mason has pointed out, the 'Declaration' asserting his title did not reflect a new imperial ideology, but referred back to a 'thoroughly medieval view' of Anglo-Scottish relations.[7]

(i)   Wars against France, 1509–50

No sooner had Henry inherited the throne than it became obvious that war against France was at the top of his agenda. As early as November 1509 the Venetian ambassador in London heard talk that the existing Anglo-French peace would not last long, while on 6 December he described the new king as 'eager for war with the king of France'. Among Henry's earliest actions were arrangements to build up England's military strength, and within a year he had ordered Calais to be reinforced, commissioned the construction of new ships, and combed Europe for armour and artillery. But as yet Henry had neither motive nor means to fight. In early January 1510, Louis XII paid the instalment of the pension owed to Henry by the terms of the 1492 Treaty of Étaples, thereby removing a potential source of grievance. The French, moreover, were allied to Pope Julius II, Emperor Maximilian I, and King Ferdinand of Aragon in the League of Cambrai which had been concluded against Venice in 1508. It is also possible, though the evidence is by no means clear-cut, that some royal councillors opposed a policy of war. As a result of these circumstances and pressures, in March 1510 Henry felt obliged to renew his father's treaty with France.[8]

None the less, Henry continued in his ambitions for war. Over the next few months he tried to drive a wedge between Louis and his allies, to bring an end to the war against Venice, and to create a new coalition against France. As a result of shifting fortunes and policies in Italy, his diplomatic efforts proved successful, and on 13 November 1511 he joined a Holy League, formed by the pope against France, as the ally of Julius II, Ferdinand of Aragon and the Venetians. Henry, however, was not interested in their goal of expelling the French from Italy, but was rather looking forward to the re-opening of the Hundred Years' War. Thus, although the Holy League was dedicated to the recovery of Central Italian towns which were then occupied by the French but had previously belonged to the Papal See, Henry himself was 'not...bound to give aid or send an army into Italy against such opponents, but elsewhere as he thinks best'. His aim, as his allies realized, was to attack western and northern France. Hence, on 17 November 1511 he signed a treaty with Ferdinand which agreed on an Anglo-Spanish expedition to capture Guienne on behalf of the English king.[9]

The 1512 campaign failed to enhance Henry's reputation: 'Nothing worth recording was done in these parts by the important English army', noted the chronicler, Polydore Virgil, in a classic understatement. In June 1512, an army of 12,000 men had set out under the Marquis of Dorset for the invasion of south-western France, but the army remained idle on the Spanish side of the border for several months until it returned home in a dispirited state. The English blamed the Spaniards for this debacle since Ferdinand had refused to provide aid for an expedition to attack the town of Bayonne, as originally agreed. He had demanded instead that the English troops should join his army in the kingdom of Navarre, which he had just successfully invaded. Without new instructions from his king, Dorset refused to agree to this change of plan, even though Ferdinand insisted that it would be much safer to invade France by way of Navarre. By the time that Henry did authorize this new strategy, Dorset's men, ill and demoralized, had forced him to abandon the campaign.[10] The naval war in 1512 had fared no better; during an attempt to intercept French ships off Brittany, the king's ship, the *Regent*, was lost together with its captain, Sir Thomas Knyvet, and some six hundred members of its crew.[11]

Far from being discouraged by this ignominious failure, Henry was determined to mount another campaign against his enemy. This time he planned to invade northern France in person. Practical considerations influenced his decision to head the army; by doing so, he hoped both to avoid the problems of Dorset's expedition and to demonstrate to his allies his personal commitment to the war. But his decision was also affected by his determination to prove his valour and win glory in battle. According to Polydore Virgil, Henry argued:

that it behoved him to enter upon his first military experience in so important and difficult a war in order that he might, by a single start to his martial knowledge, create such a fine opinion about his valour among all men that they would clearly understand that his ambition was not merely to equal but indeed to exceed the glorious deeds of his ancestors.[12]

Accordingly, no expense was to be spared for this venture. Henry made extravagant promises to subsidize the armies of Spain and the emperor, and spent huge sums on providing armour, weapons, ordnance, ships, victuals and land transport for his own invasion force of 30–40,000 men, an army at least three times the size of Henry V's invading force. The nobility, sharing in Henry's aspirations, readily gave their service to the king. Twenty-three noblemen went to France; all but two noblemen aged between nineteen and sixty actively participated in the 1513–14 campaigns (in Scotland or France) or were represented by their sons.[13]

By April 1513 Henry had signed up Spain, the emperor and the pope in another Holy League against Louis XII. This second attempt into France, however, also began badly. Ferdinand of Aragon pulled out of the war even before his ambassador in England had signed the treaty with Henry, and he then tried to draw his three allies into his new truce with France. The Spanish defection was detrimental to the war effort because it not only ended the possibility of another war front in the south-west, but it also sowed seeds of suspicion between Henry and Maximilian.[14] To make matters worse, a small naval engagement in April 1513 ended in disaster for England, when Henry's lord admiral, Sir Edward Howard, was killed. Howard was pursuing his own notion of honour in recklessly seeking revenge for the death of his friend Sir Thomas Knyvet and exposing himself to unnecessary danger.[15] Soon, however, the omens for a successful invasion of France improved. On 6 June 1513, Louis XII's army, which had crossed the Alps to reconquer Milan, was routed by the Swiss at the Battle of Novara. Immediately, Maximilian's enthusiasm for a war in northern France revived and he moved swiftly with a small force to join up with Henry's army, which had crossed over to Calais during the month of June and had soon planted itself before the fortress of Thérouanne. The town, a French enclave in Artois, had historical significance for Henry, since the English had taken it after the Battle of Crécy.

The 1513 war against France was fought amid a magnificent display of pageantry. In Edward Hall's lengthy descriptions of the sieges and skirmishes, the campaign seemed little more than an extension of the colourful tournaments previously held at court. Henry VIII's arrival at Calais on 30 June 1513 was a splendid occasion; his meeting with Maximilian at his camp outside Thérouanne was similarly designed to impress, as the king had 'prepared all thinges necessarie to mete with th'emperour in triumphe'. Once Thérouanne had fallen, Henry entered the city 'with great triumphe and honour' and received its keys personally from the emperor. There were even greater celebrations after the successful siege of Tournai, a citadel which Edward III had failed to take during the Hundred Years' War. On 2 October 1513 Henry entered that city at the head of a grand procession; wearing 'ryche armure', mounted on a horse decorated with the arms of England, and under a canopy also bearing his arms. In the spirit of many a medieval king, Henry publicly knighted his most 'valiant' esquires. To parade his victory, Henry then invited Maximilian's sister, the regent of the Low Countries, and his grandson, the Archduke Charles, to his new conquest, where he entertained them for ten days with jousts, banquets and dances.[16]

Henry's honour was thus satisfied. Although his army had not engaged in any pitched battle, it had successfully besieged two French citadels, both symbols of England's military role and reputation in the Hundred Years' War. In addition, his troops had secured a small victory over a French cavalry force on 26 August 1513; although initially the fighting had been described by Henry as a 'skirmish', it soon became elevated into a major victory, entitled the Battle of the Spurs, and great pride was taken in the number of French standards and nobles captured. Henry's taste for war, however, had been stimulated rather than sated by his military success, and consequently he looked forward to a further campaign and greater victories in the following year. Only the mediation of Pope Leo X, the defections of his allies and the generous terms offered by Louis XII persuaded him to make peace in August 1514. The peace treaty with France brought Henry some short-term rewards: Tournai was to stay in English hands and Princess Mary, Henry's younger sister, was married to the King of France and crowned in a magnificent ceremony at St Denis Cathedral.

All changed, however, in January 1515 when Louis died. His successor, the twenty-year-old Francis I, was as dedicated to war as Henry himself and determined to secure the return of Tournai from England as well as the conquest of Milan from the emperor and Navarre from Spain. None the less, between 1515 and 1522 Henry remained at peace with France, even at the cost of surrendering Tournai in 1518. The same year he also became the champion of international peace in Europe by sponsoring the Treaty of London, which upheld the principle of universal and perpetual peace. The treaty arose out of two simultaneous initiatives: first, a call from Pope Leo X for a five-year truce between Christian princes as a preliminary to a crusade against the Turks; second, peace overtures from Francis who wanted the return of Tournai and England's neutrality in a future war against Spain. In July 1518 Cardinal Campeggio, the papal legate, rode into London and announced Leo's project for a crusade to Henry; the same month the Admiral of France led an embassy to Henry's court to discuss both a treaty with England and a more general peace which would encompass the pope and other princes. By the end of September, the informal Anglo-French talks had made sufficient progress for the negotiations to be put on an official level and terms were shortly agreed.[17] The Treaty of London was in fact two separate accords. Representatives of England and France signed a treaty of universal peace on 2 October 1518 and a specifically Anglo-French agreement two days afterwards. The latter restored Tournai to Francis in return for an indemnity of 600,000 gold *écus* and arranged a marriage between Henry's two-year-old daughter Mary and the *dauphin*. The former was the first stage in a general European treaty which would eventually include Charles of Spain, Maximilian, Pope Leo and over twenty lesser powers. Each was to sign a pact with England which committed him to uphold perpetual peace and defend any party to the treaty who came under attack. By placing himself at the pivot of this treaty and presenting himself as the main arbiter of peace, Henry carved out for himself a dominant role in European politics. At a more personal level he also upstaged Francis; the French king might have proved himself the master of war, but war was now outlawed under the auspices of the English king.

During 1520 Henry remained publicly committed to the principles of the Treaty of London and tried to resolve conflicts between his new allies. At that time, Francis and Charles, now Holy Roman Emperor (see Chart 1), were drifting inexorably towards war over their rival claims to the duchy of Milan, but a new outbreak of hostilities would of course destroy Henry's reputation as an international peace-maker. The king, therefore, needed to take direct action to preserve the Treaty of London. This he tried to do in his public celebrations of amity and private interviews with both princes in the late spring of 1520, his meeting with Charles in England and with Francis in northern France. On the other hand, even then Henry conceded that his efforts at peace might fail; and, since he had no wish to be reduced to a mere onlooker in any future war in Western Europe, he signed an agreement with Charles which might pave the way to a future military alliance against France, although he rejected an imperial proposal for an immediate league. By mid-1521, however, it became clear that open war between Francis and Charles was inevitable. In May, French troops had invaded and conquered Spanish Navarre, and in response, the emperor had appealed to Henry for help under the Treaty of London and seemed desperate for an English alliance against France. There now seemed to be little point in Henry continuing to act as a neutral mediator and honest peace-broker. Indeed, it would be detrimental to do so. The last thing Henry wanted was to be stranded as the upholder of a peace-treaty which was being flagrantly violated by the other main signatories. Furthermore, upholding the Treaty of London might well end in disaster for him. If Charles's army successfully drove out the French from Navarre, if it went on to invade France, and if Francis then appealed for assistance as the victim of aggression, Henry might find himself required by the treaty's terms to prop up his rival against the more powerful Charles V. Far from wishing to uphold the principle of balance of power in the interests of European peace or English security, the very idea of helping the weaker state against the stronger was anathema to Henry, who wanted to be sure of fighting on the winning side.[18]

For these reasons, Henry sent Wolsey abroad in August 1521 to negotiate an imperial alliance. It had to be an undercover operation, since Henry would lose face were he seen to be abandoning the Treaty of London at such an early stage. Thus, under 'colour' of arbitrating in the Franco-Imperial disputes, Wolsey first attended a conference at Calais, where he heard the grievances of both sides, and then openly proceeded to Bruges to meet the emperor for further talks. There, after hard bargaining, they signed a secret offensive alliance on 25 August, which committed England to declare war against France the next year and to join his ally in a full-scale invasion of France before March 1523. In return, Charles was to marry Henry's daughter, Mary, then aged five, and to pay Henry's French pension until he had reconquered territory to that value.[19] After the treaty was signed Wolsey returned to Calais to resume peace talks with the French. He was keen to retain his credibility as a mediator so that Henry would later be able to claim that he was entering the war as defender of the Treaty of London. The imperial alliance was a diplomatic triumph for Wolsey. He had been treated with great honour at Charles V's court and had rescued his master from a difficult political situation. As he himself is said to have declared: thanks to this accord 'my sayed soveraigne lorde to his honor may lefully spred his baner and make warre in defence of his frende'.[20] Furthermore, the plans for a joint invasion of France initially looked set to provide Henry with an excellent opportunity to win glory in a new war. The conquest of France was hardly expected, but both king and minister could hope for some grand military success which would force Francis into a humiliating treaty.[21]

In May 1522 Henry's herald delivered his master's declaration of war to Francis. In the same month, the Earl of Surrey led 15,000 men out of Calais in raids on the countryside of Picardy. In the spirit of Edward III's *chevauchée* (horseback raids), his aim was to provoke a battle, but the French would not oblige and his only achievement was showing up the enemy as too faint-hearted to fight.[22] In marked contrast to the 1513 French campaign, however, neither Wolsey nor Henry had much enthusiasm for a Continental war in 1522. Admittedly they made great efforts to prepare for it, but they also frequently expressed their reservations about the enterprise. In particular, they grew increasingly suspicious that the emperor would let them down and fail to support the projected invasion of France. Their main hope came to be that Francis might capitulate quickly and sign a humiliating treaty. In August 1523, however, their mood changed with the news of the treason of the constable of France, Charles, Duke of Bourbon. His rebellion was expected to bring severe disruption to the French army and widespread assistance to an invading force, comparable to that given to Henry V by the Duke of Burgundy around the time of the Battle of Agincourt. Excited by the prospect of a victorious campaign, Henry signed a treaty with Charles V and Bourbon in July 1523, which committed them all to an immediate invasion of France. The campaign of 1523 proved to be a terrible disappointment. Initially, it went very well. In the expectation that Bourbon was planning to attack Paris from the east and that Charles V was pinning down the French army in Italy and south-west France, Henry ordered his lieutenant, the Duke of Suffolk, to join up with Flemish reinforcements and march his 11,000 soldiers towards the capital. By the end of October, the invading army was within fifty miles of Paris, having captured on the way eight towns, whose inhabitants had sworn allegiance to Henry as King of France. This was the deepest English penetration into France since the days of Henry V, and on hearing of it, an elated Henry VIII began to think that there was 'likelihood of his obtaining his ancient right to the French Crown to his singular comfort and eternal honour'. Bad news, however, soon followed. Bourbon's help and Charles's invasion of France from Spain failed to materialize. The pressure on Paris was therefore lifted and Suffolk was forced to retreat. This military reverse turned into a virtual rout owing to both the freak weather conditions of that November and the unilateral decision of the Flemish commander to disband his troops.[23]

Despite this failure, Henry did not lose faith in either Suffolk or the strategy of invading France. None the less, he did lose confidence in the value of the imperial friendship and blamed Charles V and the regent in the Netherlands for the failure of the 1523 expedition. As a result, Henry and Wolsey agreed that they would only consider another invasion if the conditions were particularly favourable. For the next eighteen months, therefore, they followed a wait-and-see policy. An alternative approach was not easy to find. Henry could hardly desert his ally without losing honour as well as leaving England isolated in Europe; while returning to a policy of championing peace was also problematic, as secret talks with the French in 1524 had revealed.[24]

A 'window of opportunity' opened in early spring 1525. On 9 March, news reached London of the great imperial victory over Francis I at the Battle of Pavia, and immediately the council discussed plans for an invasion of France. As great financial sacrifices were to be demanded of Henry's subjects, the council made enormous efforts to win their support for the war. Thus, for propaganda reasons, celebrations of the French defeat were held within the city of London, where High Mass and a *Te Deum* were sung and bonfires lit, 'with vessells of wyne at everie fier for the people to drinke'. These were soon followed by royal attempts to encourage victory processions and bonfires further afield. At the same time, Henry made appeals to his taxpayers that they should uphold his honour by supporting his bid to win back the throne of France, warning them that failure to take advantage of the occasion would lose him the esteem of all other princes. The taxpayers, however, did not heed his call. Even in 1523 and 1524, the government had experienced some difficulties in extracting a forced loan, but now there was active resistance.[25] At the same time, Charles V rejected Henry's proposal for a joint expedition to dismember France and repudiated his marriage contract with Princess Mary. To his disgust, Henry was thereby denied any benefit from the imperial victory at Pavia.

In these circumstances it was not difficult for Wolsey to persuade the king to change allies and the direction of his policy. On 30 August 1525 Henry signed five treaties, known as the Treaty of the More, with France, and over the next months English diplomatic activity encouraged the formation of the anti-imperial League of Cognac (1526), comprising the papacy, the main north Italian states and France. The aim here was not to restore 'the balance of power' in order to provide for England's defence, rather it was to re-instate Henry as a major figure in international affairs: to set him up as a mediator with Charles V who would be forced to sit down at a peace conference presided over by the English king and Wolsey.[26] Over the next year, however, the emphasis in English foreign policy shifted. While Henry continued to work towards recovering an active role in international politics, he was also concerned with securing an annulment of his marriage to Catherine of Aragon. This latter goal required the removal of the imperial army from the Italian peninsula to relieve Habsburg pressure on the pope after the sack of Rome (1527). In the event, both strands in Henry's policy were to fail. In June 1529, Pope Clement decided 'to become an Imperialist, and to live and die as such', and he signed the Treaty of Barcelona with Charles V; in August, Francis and Charles signed the bipartite peace of Cambrai which left England isolated.[27]

From 1529 until the early 1540s, Henry was too preoccupied with Reformation politics and dynastic defence to consider asserting his honour on the battlefields of Europe. For a time, Anglo-French amity survived the 'betrayal' at Cambrai because Henry needed Francis's support in the annulment case. Increasingly, however, political grievances began to sour their relationship, and it seemed that Henry might in fact abandon the French alliance in 1536, after the death of Catherine of Aragon and execution of Anne Boleyn had removed one major source of tension with the emperor. War against Francis, however, did not break out until 1543. Although Henry had been negotiating with Charles V since 1540, it was only in February 1543 that they signed the Treaty of Mutual Aid, which provided for a joint invasion of France. Towards the end of June, Henry delivered an ultimatum to the French which threatened war unless certain impossible conditions were met.

Henry's decision to return to a policy of war is explicable in both personal and political terms. At a psychological level, the king had recently suffered serious injury to his self-esteem and manhood: the impotence experienced during the Cleves marriage and the cuckoldry inflicted by Catherine Howard evidently touched him deeply. In these personal circumstances, war seemed a highly attractive option, providing the means to recapture a feeling of youth, vitality and virility. In this context it is significant that the king mustered some 40,000 men, creating the largest army to be sent abroad in England's history, one clearly designed for show rather than utility. It is also significant that despite his ulcerated leg and obese body Henry decided to join the expedition personally in 1544. At the same time, too, there were political opportunities to exploit. Charles V tried to persuade Henry that the mere existence of an Anglo-Imperial alliance might force Francis to make concessions such as the payment of the arrears of pension he owed to the King of England. Moreover, if war broke out, as seemed more than likely, there was good hope of territorial gains. By this time, Henry had set his sights upon grabbing land close to Calais, rather than co-operating with the emperor in a co-ordinated assault. As his treasury was full with the spoils from the dissolved monasteries, he had every reason to hope that the resources were available for a long campaign which could bring him territorial prizes.[28]

Although the original plan of campaign had been that both monarchs should head straight for Paris, it soon became obvious that Henry preferred to extend the Calais Pale by attacking towns in Picardy. To Charles he expressed concerns about the expense and logistical difficulties of marching deep into France, but he was also suspicious that the emperor might let him down as he had in 1523. His commanders in France reinforced his decision. The Duke of Norfolk, who landed at Calais in June 1544, advised a siege of Montreuil 'which they cannot assure us of winning, but are not in despair therof', while Sir John Russell urged attacks on Boulogne and Ardres. As Russell confided to Sir Anthony Browne:

> And in case we should after this sort wander, as I may well call it, in a wild war, dispending so much, to the King's no little charge, the same cannot sound so much to his Highness' honor; besides that to be bruited in the world that no noble and prudent a prince, the father of all Christendom in this world, as he is, and so reputed and taken, should return home without winning anything.[29]

Evidently Henry agreed, for even before he had set out for Calais he had decided to besiege both Boulogne and Montreuil.

The siege of Boulogne retrieved Henry's sense of honour. The town was so battered by ordnance that, according to Edward Hall, not one house remained standing. On 18 August Henry entered Boulogne 'like a noble and valyant conqueror'. The victory celebrations, however, remained muted. Although Henry knighted some of his comrades in arms, no jousts nor banquets were held as they had been some thirty-one years before, after the capture of Tournai. The siege of Montreuil, moreover, was a failure and it had to be raised after a relief force led by the *dauphin* moved towards the town.[30] To make matters worse, Charles V abandoned his ally and made a unilateral peace with France (Treaty of Crépy) on the very day Henry took Boulogne. This peace left Henry on the defensive. For the remainder of the war against France, his aims were to secure his own realm from attack and to hold on to the prize of Boulogne.

It soon became obvious that the expense of keeping Boulogne was too high. The war against France, which continued on land and at sea, was also proving inordinately expensive, but peace was elusive. Francis refused to agree to a treaty which would leave his territory indefinitely in English hands, while Henry was just as determined to take his new conquest with him to the grave and refused to listen to his councillors' pleas for peace at virtually any price. Eventually, however, a compromise was reached which left Henry's honour dented but intact. By the Treaty of the Campe in June 1546, Boulogne was to remain in Henry's possession until 1554, by which time the French would have paid him for it £600,000 in arrears of his pension. Henry was probably persuaded that he had given nothing away; William Paget for one argued that the eight-year occupation of Boulogne was equivalent to full title to it.[31]

The death of Henry VIII the following January nullified the arrangement at Campe. Francis himself died a few months afterwards and his successor, Henry II, was totally unwilling to continue paying the pension and equally committed to securing the immediate return of Boulogne. Had it not been for Charles V's victory over the Lutheran princes at Mühlburg, Henry would have begun an immediate assault against the English in Picardy. Fear that Charles would re-open war against France and support England continued to restrain Henry over the next two years. He reversed his policy, however, after he had heard news of the 1549 risings in England and received an assurance from Charles that he would remain neutral in any Anglo-French conflict. In August 1549, therefore, Henry II declared war on England and invaded the Boulogne region in person. Bad weather, however, hampered his progress and prevented the recapture of Boulogne during what was left of the campaigning season.[32]

Despite this reprieve, the English government was unable to cope with both the cost of defending Boulogne and fighting the French in Scotland. Consequently, by 1550 the Earl of Warwick and some of his fellow councillors were ready to abandon Henry VIII's conquest in return for peace. Some historians have viewed the Anglo-French treaty of 1550 as a total humiliation and loss of honour for England; after all, the English dropped their demands for the arrears in the pension and surrendered Boulogne for a payment of only £133,333, far less than the sum agreed in 1546. None the less, as unfavourable as the terms were, they were the best that the English government could expect from Henry II who held the whip hand in the negotiations. As Paget wrote to Warwick, the treaty might have been improved 'if peace and war had been so indifferent of us as we might have adventured sometime to have broken off [the negotiations]', but the state of the English economy and social unrest precluded a continuation of the war. The peace treaty, moreover, was not entirely a French *diktat*: Henry was forced to compromise and modify some of his original extreme demands, while the English were saved from formally signing away their rights to the French pension. In England a brave front was put on the treaty. In the city of London and Westminster, bonfires, drinking and a *Te Deum* were organized to celebrate the peace; at court, the French commissioners were treated to banquets, feasts and entertainments.[33] The following year, a large embassy of noblemen and knights arrived in France to bestow the Order of the Garter on Henry II and arrange a marriage between his daughter, Elizabeth de Valois, and Edward VI.

(ii)   Peace-time Competition

Honour and reputation did not depend entirely on military success. Recognition of repute and esteem in peace-time conditions was equally important. All this was on a personal basis between monarchs, and it frequently involved them in competitiveness with their peers over ceremonial displays at court, the entertainment of foreign embassies and the exchange of extravagant gifts. During Henry VIII's reign this normal competitiveness was heightened when the accessions of Francis and Charles introduced a strong edge of personal rivalry into international relations. For thirty-two years Henry and Francis were determined to outdo each other in exemplifying the contemporary model of kingship: in their generosity and hospitality, and in their roles as warriors and patrons of the arts. Henry's rivalry with Charles was less intense; none the less the English king deeply resented and coveted the status associated with the imperial title held by the Habsburg prince.[34]

Francis won the first round in the fight for honour and reputation by the traditional means of victory in battle. In September 1515, his army defeated the Swiss at the Battle of Marignano and he entered Milan in triumph. Hearing the news, Henry was said to be 'much grieved'. Although he made no official break with France, over the next year the king's agents were active in subsidizing the Swiss and trying to build up an anti-French league to include Spain, the pope and the emperor. Henry lost out here too, when Charles, the new King of Spain, made peace with Francis in the 1516 Treaty of Noyon and Maximilian followed suit at the beginning of 1517. Henry was thus left in humiliating isolation, excluded and betrayed by his fellow monarchs, his diplomacy in tatters.[35] The 1518 Treaty of London was therefore a magnificent coup which brought Henry right back onto the centre stage of international politics. Thanks largely to the opportunism and diplomacy of Thomas Wolsey, Henry became celebrated as the peace-maker of Europe, and London acted as the host of a magnificent international occasion. Henry's diplomatic success was marked with feasts, music, dancing, tournaments and a pageant symbolizing the five potentates (the Kings of England, France, and Spain, the pope, and the emperor) united in one league against the enemies of Christendom. Richard Pace, Henry's secretary, gave an oration on peace, three versions of which were published under official sanction. All in all, the king spent an estimated £9600 on the occasion, an unusually high sum even for Henry VIII to devote to court festivities.[36]

Although the Treaty of London retrieved Henry's international reputation, it did not mark an end to his rivalry with Francis. There was outward courtesy, even friendly exchanges, between the two monarchs, but an underlying yet unmistakable competitiveness lay between them. Despite French irritation, in February 1519 Henry refused to allow the Marechal de Châtillon to enter Tournai with banners and trumpets, as 'the cytie was neither yelded nor gotten but delivered for confederacion of mariage'.[37] Soon afterwards, Henry decided to stand against Francis and Charles as a third candidate in the imperial election of 1519. His intervention was partly prompted by an unwillingness to sit back idly and risk the French king's victory in the contest; but, in addition, his honour demanded that he should compete on equal terms with the Kings of France and Spain for this august title. After all, contemporaries recognized that 'the Emperor is the chief of all Christian princes' and 'should be chosen from the greatest kings of Christendom'.[38]

Similarly, if less ambitiously, Henry was determined to prove himself the equal of 'so hygh princes', first during his personal interviews with Francis and Charles (elected Emperor Charles V in 1519) in the late spring of 1520, and later when Charles visited him in London in 1522. For a few days in May 1520, Henry played host to Charles at Dover and Canterbury where he made a special point of demonstrating their intimacy as kinsmen. Immediately afterwards, the king accompanied some 6000 of his court to Guisnes for the meeting with Francis, known as the Field of Cloth of Gold. This was a far more elaborate affair, a grand chivalric spectacle, where in the name of peace the two kings competed in the grandeur of their courts and the prowess of their men at arms.[39] In June, Henry met again with Charles, this time in Flanders, where he was entertained royally. Yet, for all their ostentatious display, serious politics underlay these high-level meetings of 1520. For Henry and Wolsey, their purpose was to lock Charles and Francis into their pledges to maintain peace in Europe. On their side, however, both rulers (but more particularly Charles) hoped to use the meetings to reach a closer understanding with Henry and turn him from an impartial mediator into an active ally. Two years later at a meeting with Charles in London, Henry again seized the opportunity for an ostentatious display of power designed to dazzle his guest and make a serious point. By the terms of the 1521 Treaty of Bruges, the emperor was obligated to visit the English court the following year as a preliminary or signal for Henry to declare war on France. Accordingly, at the end of May 1522, Charles arrived on the south coast, and was accompanied to London by eighteen English noblemen. Their ceremonial entry into the city was marked by pageants, some of which were designed to assert the equality in status between the English king and the Holy Roman Emperor; one, for example, drew attention to Henry's descent from King Arthur who according to legend had held imperial power over the British Isles, Scandinavia and Gaul. By devices such as this, Henry was announcing that he was not the junior partner in the joint enterprise against France. Over the next month, Charles was treated to a round of tournaments, banquets and hunts, but time was also found for negotiations. Two treaties were concluded which postponed the invasion of France for a year and laid down the details of military strategy.[40]

The war against France between 1522 and 1525 revealed to Henry the total unreliability of his imperial ally. Not surprisingly, therefore, the king and Wolsey abandoned the emperor and made a unilateral peace with France which lasted until the late 1530s. Outward friendship, however, masked the continuing rivalry between the two kings and competition over status and image. As Glenn Richardson has explained, their cultural interaction 'was designed to assert superior international status through every means other than military confrontation. It was conducted through magnificent ritualistic displays of royal friendship.' When the two rulers met at Boulogne and Calais in October 1532, each tried to outdo the other in the lavish entertainments provided and the extravagance of the gifts exchanged. In addition, for the rest of his reign Henry built up vast collections of plate, tapestries, books, manuscripts and armour in an attempt to match the magnificent palaces and libraries of his far richer and more fashionable rival.[41]

Henry's rivalry with Francis lasted until both died in early 1547. It was a unique royal relationship which had an important impact both on England's foreign policy and cultural development. Thereafter, competitiveness between European rulers continued but was usually more detached and impersonal. The only exception was the rivalry which developed between Elizabeth I and Mary Queen of Scots in the mid-1560s but was prematurely curtailed by the forced abdication of the latter in 1567. To assert her superiority, Elizabeth tried to outdo her younger cousin in the courtly style and arts expected of a Renaissance princess: beauty, grace, music and dancing; hence her famous interviews in 1564 with Mary's envoy, Sir James Melville, where she attempted to show off her fashionable gowns and musical talents, subjecting him also to insistent inquiries about the comparative appearance and accomplishments of herself and his mistress. The preparations for Elizabeth's meeting with Mary at Nottingham or York in 1562 (cancelled because of England's impending war against France) make clear that the English queen intended to impress her rival with masques, tilts and pageants. Each queen plied the other with gifts of portraits, miniatures, jewels and verse, although Elizabeth's parsimony limited the scale of the ritual exchanges. At all times, Elizabeth asserted her seniority over Mary: counselling her whom to marry and offering advice on policy. As Queen of Scotland in her own right, dowager Queen of France and heiress presumptive to the English throne, Mary deeply resented Elizabeth's attitude. The mutual personal antagonism which increasingly marked their relationship made agreement between them difficult to reach on important areas of potential conflict and adversely affected Anglo-Scottish relations between 1561 and 1567.[42]

(iii)   The Scottish Wars, 1509–50

Historians usually focus on border raids and security concerns as the political realities which dominated Anglo-Scottish relations in the six-teenth-century.[43] While their importance is undeniable and will be dealt with in Chapter 3, the issue of honour is here given its due weight as an influence on the foreign policy of both realms before 1550. Underlying the tensions between the two royal houses of Tudor and Stewart were: Henry VIII's treatment of the Scottish king as the junior partner ruling the British Isles; his claim that Scotland was a feudal dependency of the Crown of England; and his assertion that the Scottish king owed him homage. Not surprisingly, the Scots felt 'despised' by the English and deeply resented their claims to superiority.[44] The Scottish kings, James IV and James V, meanwhile, were determined to prove them-selves the equal of Henry VIII, capable for instance of pursuing an independent foreign policy. Indeed, their attempts to continue the 'Auld Alliance' and extend the French connection should be seen in this light.

At the beginning of the sixteenth century, Anglo-Scottish relations were fairly harmonious. In 1502 James IV signed the Treaty of Perpetual Peace with Henry VII and a year later married his elder daughter, Margaret. The treaty worked well and James was keen to keep peace with England on Henry VIII's accession; therefore, he immediately renewed the Perpetual Treaty and agreed to measures designed to settle outstanding border disputes. At the same time, however, James was determined to keep a free hand in foreign policy, and consequently both maintained his former contacts with Louis XII and continued his con-struction of a well-equipped, modern navy with French support. Even after it became clear that Henry was planning war against France, James hoped to keep both alliances alive. For this reason, after the formation of the Holy League in 1511, he tried to use his diplomacy to reconcile Louis XII with the pope and thereby prevent a war in which he would be forced to choose between his two allies.[45]

In the event, James chose to side with France. Almost certainly his motives were closely related to the issue of his honour, for Henry consistently showed him public disrespect in the period prior to the outbreak of war. First, in 1511 Henry and James fell out over a dispute which, though relatively trivial in itself, touched upon their honour. Despite protests from England, James allowed Scottish pirates to prey on English shipping, and then complained loudly and demanded redress when Henry's lord admiral and sea captains dealt with them peremptorily, killing the most notorious, Andrew Barton. In this episode both monarchs believed their honour and reputation were at stake and refused to compromise. By the end of 1511 James was claiming to the pope that the 1502 treaty was void in the light of Henry's treatment of Scottish citizens and glaring disregard of the treaty's terms.[46] Second, in his attempts to keep James neutral in the imminent war against France, Henry resorted to intimidation and insults, behaviour which deeply irked the Scottish king. Hearing rumours that the Scots intended to invade the North as soon as the English army set off for France, Henry sent Nicholas West, Dean of Windsor, to Scotland in February 1513 to demand a written guarantee of neutrality from James. To extract this promise, West uttered blunt threats of reprisal if James broke with Henry. James's response was to send back to Henry an equally unconciliatory message, calling on him to give up the invasion of France and demanding just reparation for the 'undeniable outrages' of the English against his realm. In truth, James was in a quandary. He had no wish for war against England nor a rupture with the pope, but he was unwilling to submit to the English king. Perhaps had Henry offered to pay pensions in return for his neutrality and if West had conducted the negotiations with more blandishments and fewer threats, James might have stayed out of the war; but Henry's obvious lack of respect for his brother-in-law, coming after renewed English claims of overlordship in the parliament of 1512, offended the honour of the Scots and their king. Consequently, only a few weeks after West had returned home, James agreed with Louis XII that he would send an army over the border into England and his fleet to France as soon as Henry VIII had departed for Calais. In return he requested the presence of 2000 French soldiers in Scotland for defence. At the end of July 1513, he summoned his lords to muster for an invasion of Northumberland and despatched his Lyon Herald to deliver an ultimatum to Henry at his camp outside Thérouanne.[47]

Before setting off for France with the bulk of his army and nobles, Henry had left his border relatively well defended with troops mustered under the generalship of the Earl of Surrey, but he still seemed surprised by James's sudden ultimatum and attack. Furious at James's 'dishonourable demeanour' in breaking faith with him, Henry ordered his herald to accuse him of rebellion in taking up arms against his overlord. Meanwhile, Catherine of Aragon, ruling England in Henry's absence, raised a large army to combat the invading force. All went well for the English troops, which annihilated the Scots at the Battle of Flodden on 9 September. Less was made of this victory than those at Thérouanne and Tournai; after all, Henry himself had not commanded the army that had slain the Scottish king and most of his aristocracy.[48] Henry, however, could still play out the role of the honourable knight, and he requested from the pope that the excommunication of James be lifted so that his body could be buried in St Paul's Cathedral: 'considering his own kingly dignity...considering also that honour demands it'.[49]

Scotland excited little interest in the English king thereafter. He made no attempt to control the realm, despite the opportunities that were afforded by the minority government of James V, the position of Margaret Tudor as queen-mother, and the feuds tearing apart the Scottish nobility. Henry believed his reputation depended on success on the European stage and not in dominating his neighbour. His main concerns, therefore, were to keep Scotland weak and unthreatening, and to stop Francis I from rebuilding the 'Auld Alliance' during the years when England was at war against France.

It was only in the late 1530s when James V seemed to be following in the steps of his father and seeking an independent foreign policy that Henry viewed Scotland once again as a danger and its king as a precocious rival who had to be brought to heel. At first Henry approached his young nephew gently; he gave him avuncular advice and tried to arrange a personal interview with him. Despite this, James continued to go his own way. In 1537 he accepted a consecrated cap and sword from the pope, who had excommunicated Henry; in 1538 he took, as his second French wife, Mary of Guise, who had just previously rejected the suit of Henry himself; and he consistently resisted Henry's requests for a personal meeting, only agreeing in 1540 to a three-way summit which would include France. While James's conduct increasingly alarmed Henry, it also offended him, especially when he was kept waiting for two weeks at York in the summer of 1541 in the expectation that James would visit him there. Henry's words in the later declaration of war against James have a distinct ring of sincerity: 'we be in dedes so injured, contempned and despised, as we ought not with sufferaunce to pretermitte and passe over'.[50]

It was largely fear that James could not be trusted to remain neutral during his projected campaign against France that led Henry to turn to strong-arm tactics in the summer of 1542; but the resort to heavy threats backed up by force also arose from his desire to teach his young nephew a lesson. To bully the Scots into submission, Henry issued them with a tough ultimatum: either they would give immediate pledges that James would come into England to conclude a treaty of amity, or else the English army would do 'some notable exploit in Scotland' and carry out 'some honourable enterprise...to make them feel their fault'. While the Scots hesitated, Henry ordered his army under the Duke of Norfolk to raid the borders. At the same time, he issued a proclamation of war which reiterated his claim to the overlordship of Scotland and his right to receive the homage and fealty of the Scottish king. This action, however, stung James into retaliation. He immediately mustered his men, appealed to Rome and France, and on 23 November led an army of some 18,000 men across the border on the way to invading the West Marches. His troops, however, were soon put to flight at Solway Moss, leaving behind on the field of battle some 1200 prisoners, including two earls, five barons and five hundred lairds and gentlemen. Twenty-one of them were brought down to London and paraded through the city streets on their way to the Tower. On the 21 December they were dressed in their most impressive clothes 'new gownes of blake damaske furred with blacke conyes and cottes of blacke velvet', and then they rode on horseback to Westminster for a festive Christmas. On 27 December they went to Greenwich where they swore before Henry 'to sett forth this Majesti's tytle that he had to the realme of Scotland'.[51]

This public humiliation of the Scots satisfied Henry's honour. The death of James V (possibly from nervous exhaustion) in December 1542, which left his week-old daughter as queen, provided Henry with another opportunity to dominate Scotland but, as in 1514, he refused to take it. His heart was set on glory in France not an Anglo-Scottish Union. His plan, therefore, was to set off with his army to Calais, leaving behind the Earl of Arran, governor of Scotland during the regency of Mary Stewart, to rule as a stooge in the interests of the English Crown. This policy might have been successful, had Henry shown some sensitivity towards the Scots and respected their fears that a marriage between Mary and his son, Edward, might end with an attempted annexation of their realm. Instead, Henry wanted to assert his control over Scotland by demanding Mary's presence in England, seizing Scottish shipping, and bullying Arran into delivering Scottish castles south of the Forth into English hands.

At first it appeared that Henry's heavy-handed approach had worked. On 1 July 1543 the Scots agreed to the Treaties of Greenwich which contracted the marriage between Queen Mary and Prince Edward. Not surprisingly, Henry and his Council were convinced that 'the Governor and Lords of Scotland have wholly submitted', but their confidence was misguided. In September Arran deserted the English cause and joined up with the pro-French party led by Cardinal Beaton. The earl had never been a true supporter of the Anglo-Scottish marriage and union, but had needed time to consolidate his political position before showing his cards. The surviving leaders of the pro-English faction were powerless to prevent the Scottish parliament from repudiating the Treaties of Greenwich in December 1543 and renewing all former treaties with France.[52] By the spring of 1544 Henry realized that his Scottish clients were in no position to return Scotland to the satellite status he demanded. Outraged by what he saw as the treachery of his sworn allies, he ordered the destruction and spoil of Edinburgh, Leith and St Andrews, 'as there may remain forever a perpetual memory of the vengeance of God lightened upon [them] for their falsehood and disloyalty'. He rejected, however, the recommendation of his commander-in-chief, Edward Seymour Earl of Hertford, that the army should occupy some strategic towns, since he had no wish to tie up a large army in Scotland. As Hertford had suspected, one raid was not enough to intimidate the Scots, who were strengthened by French money and an expeditionary force. The years 1544 and 1545 witnessed a number of brutal raids, which the government presented as great victories, despite their lack of efficacy; in London, bonfires were lit and a *Te Deum* sung at St Paul's in celebration both on 22 May 1544 and 24 September 1545.[53]

With Henry VIII's death, English policy towards Scotland changed. The man in charge of England in 1547 was Seymour, now promoted to be Lord Protector and Duke of Somerset, and his one *idée fixe* was Scotland. Like Henry, he was greatly influenced by his honour and reputation in seeking to crush the Scots; but, unlike the late king, he may also have been influenced by religious ideology in his desire for the union of the two realms. He had long been convinced that periodic strikes across the border were as futile as they were expensive. He intended, instead, to subdue the Scots permanently by arranging the marriage between Queen Mary and Edward VI and establishing a 'pale' within Scotland, an area controlled by heavily fortified English garrisons. Before he had time to muster and deploy his army, however, a French fleet moved quickly and unexpectedly to capture St Andrew's Castle from its pro-English Protestant occupants. This left Somerset with no English centre of power within Scotland and improved the morale of the Scottish lords. Perhaps for this reason, very few Scots responded to Somerset's call to join with the English, honour the marriage compact of 1543, and repudiate both Rome and the French alliance. On the contrary, most gathered under Arran's banner. At the Battle of Pinkie on 10 September 1547, the Scottish force probably comprised some 23,000 men while the English army was somewhere between 15,000 and 19,000 strong.[54]

The Scottish defeat at Pinkie was devastating; estimates of the casualties vary, but probably about 6000 Scots were killed compared to only 600 on the English side. The English superiority in cavalry and artillery helps explain the scope of their victory, but the Scottish effort was hampered by inadequate training of their pikemen and the poor leadership of their commanders. The battle did not, however, result in the subjugation of Scotland. Although Somerset was able to establish a ring of garrisons in the south of the country, he proved unable to take Edinburgh or extend his control beyond the Tay. The English garrisons, moreover, frequently came under attack from the Scots and proved to be very expensive to maintain. To make matters even worse, 6000 French troops arrived at Leith in June 1548 to help the Scots. In July the Scottish parliament agreed to accept French protection against the 'cruelties, depredations and intolerable injuries done by our old enemies of England'; in August, Mary was sent to France; and after the fall of Haddington Castle in September, the English were on the military defensive.

The wars in Scotland, together with the short war in northern France, proved too much for the English treasury. The Scottish war alone cost £580,393 between 1547 and 1549. Thus, once Somerset had fallen from power in October 1549, the emphasis in English foreign policy changed dramatically. Despite his military reputation, the Earl of Warwick, the new effective ruler of England, was a realist who recognized the necessity of negotiating an end to the war in Scotland. His first offer was the restoration of Boulogne to France in return for a marriage between Mary and Edward VI, but the French naturally refused to accept it. At last, the English commissioners were forced to accept that Mary would remain in France and eventually marry the *dauphin*, acknowledging thereby their own loss of influence in Scotland and the renewal of the 'Auld Alliance' in a new and more dangerous form.

(iv)   A New Emphasis

During the second half of the sixteenth century, there emerged a shift of emphasis in English foreign policy. It was not that England moved away from warfare; on the contrary, between 1559 and 1603 England was at war for approximately twenty years in contrast to the fifteen years between 1509 and 1559. As already seen, one element of change was the decline in the extent of personal competitiveness between monarchs. A second concerned the rhetoric and motives behind the wars: the English monarchs seldom publicly asserted their right of suzerainty over Scotland or claim to the crown of France; apart from Calais, they spoke no more about England's ancestral lands in Normandy, Guienne or Aquitaine; in their letters, proclamations and propaganda they made rarer appeals to their personal honour. Indeed, it would appear that honour and reputation were playing a far less important role in fashioning dynastic relationships. The issues of national defence and religion were taking their place.

This change in the rhetoric and the motives behind war can already be detected in Mary I's policy towards France and Elizabeth I's so-called Newhaven Adventure of 1562–4. Mary and her Council initially had no wish to go to war against Henry II in defence of her husband's honour. Indeed, in the matrimonial treaty of 1553 it had been agreed that Philip of Spain would not draw England into the Habsburgs' existing conflict against France. At the same time, Mary had assured the French that her marriage would not interfere with the peace between them. Even when a new war broke out between France and Spain in the autumn of 1556, the English Council hoped to remain neutral. In November, couriers arrived from Philip to request English aid if the truce were broken in northern Europe in accordance with England's 1542 and 1546 treaties with the Netherlands; but in the event it took five months to convince the Council that England should go to war against France. Councillors such as Heath, Mason, Winchester, Cardinal Pole and most of the queen's household opposed the policy of war, even though Spanish pensions were distributed regularly to Mary's English advisors. In March 1557 Philip arrived in England to exert personal pressure on his wife and her Council. Even he was surprised at the degree of conciliar opposition to the war, though he was hopeful of breaking it down. On 3 April, however, a select group of councillors wrote down for him their decision that England 'ought not and could not declare war'. Mary, too, did not want war. According to the May 1557 report of the Venetian ambassador, Giovanni Michiel, who had just departed from his residency in England, the queen was trying to avoid a rupture with France and even holding back from supplying her husband with large sums of money. When at last war was declared, it was on grounds of national defence, a military response to the French-backed invasion of Thomas Stafford on Scarborough Castle in April 1557. Although the raid was small-scale and easily combatted, it demonstrated to the Council that the French king was Mary's enemy and might well attack English territory elsewhere. It was for this reason that Mary proclaimed war on 7 June 1557; significantly, her proclamation emphasized the issue of defence and made no mention of ancient claims to the French throne.[55]

Elizabeth was far more enthusiastic for war against France in 1562 than Mary had been in 1557. She was also more influenced by the concept of honour, seeing the war as an opportunity for winning back Calais, which had been militarily lost to the Crown in January 1558. The recognition of its forfeiture at the conference of Cateau-Cambrésis had been a severe blow to Elizabeth. Initially, her commissioners had been ordered to refuse to sign an agreement ceding England's sovereignty over the pale. Only when it became clear that Henry II would not surrender it without a fight and Philip II would not employ troops for its recovery, were they instructed to accept a face-saving formula, whereby the French would hold Calais for eight years and would then either return it to England or pay a sum in compensation. Consequently, Elizabeth leapt at the opportunity of sending troops to assist the Prince of Condé, leader of the Huguenots, when it appeared that he would restore Calais to her as the price for English aid. By the Treaty of Hampton Court signed on 20 September 1562, she promised to send 100,000 crowns and 6000 men to France. Half of them would be used to help Condé and the other half would garrison Le Havre and Dieppe, which would be exchanged for Calais at the end of the war.[56] None the less, neither her proclamation of war nor her propaganda during 1562 made any reference to the queen's honour or reputation; and they only mentioned her 'good ryght' to Calais in passing. Instead, the war was justified on grounds of 'the honour of God' and the issue of national security. Religion and defence were the two banners calculated to unite the political nation behind the war, rather than the prize of Calais, royal claims to the crown of France, or Elizabeth's reputation and honour.[57]

The expedition was a disaster for England. During the autumn and winter of 1562, the Huguenots endured several defeats, culminating in the capture of Condé in December. In March 1563 the prince patched up a religious peace with Catherine de Medici and promised to oust the English garrison from Le Havre. At the beginning of June 1563, French troops invested the town but the plague took it first. According to Warwick, English soldiers were dying at the rate of a hundred soldiers a day in July. By the end of the month Warwick was completely worn down and forced to surrender. After this *debâcle*, Elizabeth gave up any aspirations of winning back Calais through war. The restoration of the lost territory was, nevertheless, still quite important to her: in 1567 she unrealistically demanded its restitution in accordance with the 1559 treaty and protested that the French refusal was 'altogether unjust and unreasonable'; in 1571 she wanted to negotiate its return as part of a matrimonial treaty with the French Duke of Anjou, and only desisted after some of her councillors begged her to drop 'that Toy of Calais'. Yet, in truth, England's dynastic claims in France no longer exercised the same hold on either the queen, her councillors or the wider nobility. Indeed, when some members of the Council thought in terms of territorial expansion, their eyes turned to the Netherlands and the Spanish Empire over which the English monarch had no rights or claim. Elizabeth herself, of course, had no truck with such notions of aggrandisement.[58]

Why did this change occur? One obvious theory is that the move away from warfare as the expression of royal machismo and chivalric ideals was simply the result of two women sitting on the throne during the second half of the century. Unlike Henry VIII, his daughters would feel no imperative to win fame through proving their valour in battle. Indeed, in her 1593 speech to parliament, Elizabeth herself suggested that her preference not 'to enlarge my dominions' and 'never to invade my neighbours' stemmed from her 'womankind'.[59] Yet this explanation is unsatisfactory, if only because continental warfare in pursuit of honour and territorial gain had been discredited even before the accession of a female ruler, hence the 1550 Treaty of Boulogne. Furthermore, England did not rush into Continental warfare on the death of Elizabeth and accession of James. Another plausible explanation is that the subversive influence of new ideas was having an impact on policy. It could conceivably be argued that the chivalric concept of honour was first attacked and then displaced by both humanism and Protestantism, the two cultures which came to permeate Elizabethan England. According to this view, the Elizabethan government was dominated by legally trained civic humanists, who were distanced from chivalric ideals by birth and education and found martial values incompatible with their own ethos of peace, reform and civilian service to the commonwealth. They shared

Erasmus's derision of chivalric romances, as 'unlearned, foolish and old womanish', and agreed with Roger Ascham's condemnation of knightly feats at arms as 'open manslaughter and bold bawdry'. Protestantism, likewise, seemed to offer an alternative value system: pious Protestants equated virtue with godliness not chivalric behaviour; besides, though they were by no means pacifists, they justified war only when it was a fight against the enemies of the Lord. In this new climate of ideas it seems no wonder that national defence and religion provided the justifications for all of Elizabeth's wars.[60]

As it stands, however, there are several important problems with this explanation too. First, humanism was not the stark antithesis of late medieval chivalry, as is implied. The late Burgundian writers on chivalry looked to classical examples of the martial virtues they admired, while humanists, such as Thomas Elyot, urged that military exercises were an essential part of a gentleman's education and Castiglione's *The Book of the Courtier,* translated into English in 1561, judged that 'the first and true profession of the courtier must be that of arms...And he will win a good reputation by demonstrating these qualities.' Second, chivalric forms experienced a new lease of life in the Elizabethan period. It is certainly true that Elizabethan chivalry had a hollow centre, as more than ever before its rituals had become divorced from the realities of warfare. None the less, books on chivalry and romances enjoyed renewed popularity while, after a brief eclipse in the mid-Tudor years, tournaments were revived at court, often being held to entertain and impress foreign embassies. Foreign princes were invited to join the Order of the Garter, and they reciprocated by bestowing similar honours on some English noblemen. Chivalric concepts of honour, moreover, continued to be an important element in the thinking and code of conduct of the Elizabethan nobility and gentlemen. Challenges to duel in the cause of honour and reputation were not uncommon at court, and the Earl of Essex even challenged the governor of Rouen to fight him in single combat on a typically chivalric point of honour: 'that the king's [Henry IV of France] cause is more just than that of the [Catholic] League and that my Mistress is more beautiful than yours'.[61]

Chivalry, therefore, was not displaced by humanism and Protestantism. Instead, late medieval concepts of honour blended with Renaissance ideas of courtly behaviour and Elizabethan religious zeal and patriotism to create a new synthesis. This meant that wars were generally seen as having a higher purpose than just individual or princely honour, but at the same time the chivalric ideal and search for reputation influenced the conduct of military leaders. The military careers of both the Earl of Essex and Sir Philip Sidney illustrate this point. Throughout his campaigns in the Netherlands and France, Essex, while fighting in the name of the Protestant cause, employed the rhetoric of honour in battle and behaved in the manner of the chivalric knight. His letters home from war treated the military operations as theatres for chivalric display; for example, his descriptions of the siege of Rouen stressed the personal heroism of individual captains, discussed the capture of an enemy redoubt as a point of honour, and considered the disgrace of the enemy as a major victory. Similarly, the death of the Protestant hero and humanist poet Sir Philip Sidney, as told by his admiring friend and biographer Fulke Greville, was the model of knightly virtue. At the Battle of Zutphen, hearing the English marshall was unable to wear his thigh armour because of a recent wound, Sidney cast aside his own thigh piece in a fatal chivalric gesture. The musket ball that took his life hit Sidney in the thigh. He lingered in intense pain for three weeks, and then on the point of death gave his waterbottle to a fellow wounded comrade, though he himself was parched with thirst.[62]

As will be seen in later chapters, the Reformation was undoubtedly important in explaining the change in royal and conciliar rhetoric and policy, since it raised the issues of national defence and the godly cause as new imperatives in foreign policy. Pragmatic considerations, however, also played their part – arguably a crucial part – in explaining the drift away from wars fought largely or solely in pursuit of glory and ancient claims. The practical realities of the French and Scottish wars in the 1540s had raised large questions about England's capacity to put huge armies into the field or even to defend relatively small garrisons in Scotland and France without causing economic damage and social dislocation. The war, said the Bishop of Winchester in 1545, is 'miserie': it was hitting commerce hard and imposing heavy financial burdens on the state. Indeed, the imposition of taxes and forced loans became so resented in 1545 that two aldermen in London protested against the king's demand for a benevolence. By 1550 Paget was complaining that the war was causing inflation, 'idlenes among the people' and social unrest; and he urged peace so that 'the commyn welth & estate of the realme may be browght to a perfait & happy estate'. These kinds of arguments came to be echoed in the council meetings under Mary when entry into Philip II's war was being discussed: famine made it impossible to feed an army; rupture of trade with France would damage the economy; government finances and the threat of sedition made intervention impossible.[63] For a short time under Elizabeth in 1562, the burdens of war were forgotten as government servants united in their enthusiasm for the campaign in France, but they were soon to be reminded of them as the queen's debts mounted. What is more, the humiliating loss of Calais (1558) and the withdrawal from Le Havre (1563) not only cost huge sums – they also exposed the inadequacies of the English military machine. No longer would it be possible for England to send the cream of its aristocracy overseas at the head of a force of some 30–40,000 men. No longer could English longbows keep their reputation as superior fighting machines, when they were pitted against armies equipped with firearms and artillery. In these circumstances, war had to be treated with circumspection. For the monarch, it was a risky enterprise, no longer the opportunity for the acquisition of glory. Realists that they were, Warwick (later Northumberland), Mary I and Elizabeth I soon comprehended this political truth, and accordingly tried to refrain from warfare, at least until the cause of dynastic and national defence drew the latter two into Continental wars.

3

SECURITY AND DEFENCE

This chapter treats border defence, dynastic security and the Counter-Reformation threat in separate sections. As the sixteenth century progressed, however, all three areas became closely related. In the first place, the monarch's dynastic interests and England's national security issues began to merge after Henry VIII's break from Rome, as the threat to England from pretenders ceased to be simply dynastic in nature. Thus, in the mid and late 1530s Reginald Pole was a danger to the king because of his papal connections as well as his Yorkist lineage. Later on, the pretender Mary Queen of Scots imperilled the Protestant Church as much as the person of Elizabeth herself, and came to be treated by the pope and Philip II as a banner for the Counter-Reformation. In addition, the nature of the threat to England's land borders also changed over the period. Whereas in the first half of the century the northern borders were insecure mainly because of the Franco-Scottish 'Auld Alliance' and the Scottish king's readiness to open up a second front in the Anglo-French continental wars, the issues dominating Anglo-Scottish relations during Elizabeth's reign concerned religion and dynasty. Confronted with the complexity and interrelatedness of these dangers Elizabethans made sense of them by falling back on conspiracy theory; as far as they were concerned, all the threats to England's security were the work of a Catholic league led by the pope. Historians, however, can probably best understand them if the themes are disentangled as far as is possible, and discussed individually.

(i)   Border Defence

Unlike the Stewarts in the seventeenth century, the Tudors had many land borders to defend: the frontier with Scotland, the land around the

English parts of Ireland and, until 1558, the periphery of the Calais Pale. Militarily it was far from easy to protect frontier lands which were remote from the centre of royal power and exposed to attack. Despite their many experiments at military control, no Tudor government solved the problem, and throughout the sixteenth century English border areas remained notoriously insecure, suffering frequent raids and often slipping into war. Scottish lords raided the English borders; Gaelic chieftains attacked the English Pale and plantations in Ireland; and Scottish and French kings sent armies of invasion into northern England and the English Pale within France.[1]

There were political causes aplenty to provoke conflict and invasion scares. Anglo-Scottish and Anglo-French border relations were plagued by jurisdictional disputes and rival claims to lands. Trouble arose, for example, when fugitives from justice fled over the frontier, especially if their pursuers followed them into foreign territory. Ill-feeling was further generated if the fugitives were political refugees, as convention dictated that they were entitled to sanctuary despite demands for their extradition. Such jurisdictional conflicts were usually contained by the local administrators, but they could sometimes escalate into border violence and call for the attention of the central government. Land disputes were a still more serious source of friction. The Scots claimed Berwick, the fortress town first captured by Edward I, re-occupied by the Scots, and taken again by the English in 1482. Both kingdoms laid claim to the 'Debatable Lands', the territory where the line of the Anglo-Scottish border remained unclear (see Map 3). Along the border of the Calais Pale, there were also small-scale boundary disagreements, as for example when in 1556 England challenged the French possession of a wealthy monastery on the frontier.[2] Minor Anglo-French territorial disputes during the mid-Tudor period were, however, symptoms of a deeper problem: Henry II's resentment at an English presence on mainland France.

All these arguments created much ill-will and generated considerable diplomatic activity, but only on one occasion did they actually lead to war. This was the Anglo-Scottish war of 1532–3, which arose after Henry VIII's officials in the North laid claim to the priory and grounds of Canonbie in the Debatable Lands. Believing that James V was preparing to use force to possess it, Henry ordered a northern army over the border. His soldiers clashed with the Scots and successfully seized the Cawmills, a strip of derelict territory half a mile north of Berwick, which he at first refused to surrender. The war, however, did not last long and, after

French mediation, a peace was concluded in 1534, whereby Henry was forced to return his 'spoils of war'.[3]

Unusually, the war of 1532–3 broke out during a period of amity between the French and English kings. More commonly, Anglo-Scottish armed conflict arose at times when relations between England and France were hostile. This was because the most important cause of Anglo-Scottish armed conflict in the sixteenth century was the close relationship between France and Scotland embodied in the 'Auld Alliance', the treaty of alliance which was first ratified in 1296 and renewed by every Scottish and French monarch until 1560. Because of the 'Auld Alliance', successive French kings expected the Scots to come to their aid if England attacked France. An invasion from Scotland or trouble along the borders would compel the English government to leave a large army in the North instead of throwing all its men into a campaign against France. With this strategic advantage in mind, the French were determined to preserve the alliance and their sphere of influence in Scotland. Consequently, whenever it looked as though England might subdue the Scots by force or impose upon them a dynastic union, the French king sent financial and military aid to francophile Scottish factions. On its side, English governments understandably viewed French influence in the British Isles as a serious security threat and attempted to exclude it at every opportunity.[4] At times during the first half of the century, the French also saw advantages in causing trouble along England's other frontier, in Ireland. Henry II, in particular, developed contacts with Gaelic chieftains, in the hope of inciting rebellions and pinning down English troops in Ireland which might otherwise be used against him on the Continent. In reality, though, the threat of French intervention in Ireland was far less serious than it appeared to the alarmist English administration in Dublin or than it actually was in Scotland. None the less, it exposed Ireland's potential as a locus for foreign intrigues which was to cause legitimate concern in England during Elizabeth's reign, when both the pope and Spanish king sent troops to aid rebels against her rule.

During the reigns of Henry VIII and Edward VI the 'Auld Alliance' was unquestionably the major source of friction between the English and Scottish monarchs, although, as seen in Chapter 2, questions of honour and reputation had an important influence on their relationships. The 1513 war arose directly from the 'Auld Alliance'. On Henry VIII's accession, James IV had mistakenly believed it was possible to be the ally of both England and France, but he soon came to realize that he could not retain the friendship of both monarchs, nor remain neutral in the impending Anglo-French war. For reasons of honour he chose the French alliance. Consequently, no sooner had Henry set out for France than the Scottish king delivered him an ultimatum 'to desiste fra further invasion' or risk a war against Scotland. James then sent a fleet to assist Hugh O'Donnell, Lord of Tyrconnell, in attacking Carrick-fergus, the principal English stronghold in Ulster, and led his army into Northumberland, destroying and capturing castles near the border. The English were in fact caught somewhat unprepared, but neither of James's military actions proved successful and the Scots suffered the devastating defeat at Flodden.[5] Henry, of course, made no attempt to follow up the English victory but, even had the conquest of Scotland been his goal, it would probably have eluded him. The English army was too disorganized and the campaigning season too late for a major invasion.[6] During the 1520s, when Henry was again at war against France, Francis I also tried to use the Scots as a military distraction. He sent over to Scotland the French-born Duke of Albany, heir presumptive to the Scottish throne, with promises of armed support if the Scots invaded England. The Scottish lords, however, were unwilling to risk another calamitous defeat at the French king's bidding; in 1522 they refused to respond to Albany's call to arms; in 1523 the duke did raise an army to assault Wark Castle but it quickly retreated on hearing that an English army was approaching under the Earl of Surrey.[7]

The 'Auld Alliance' was not resurrected in a dangerous form again until the mid-1530s. From 1524 to 1528 the pro-English party in Scotland, headed by Margaret Tudor's second husband, the Earl of Angus, dominated the minority government of James V, while Francis I, embroiled in the Italian wars, failed to intervene to restore French influence at Edinburgh. By the time that Angus fell from power, moreover, Henry VIII and Francis I appeared firm friends. By the mid-1530s, however, their relationship had seriously deteriorated, and at the same time the adult James V was pursuing an aggressively pro-French policy and building up closer relations with the pope. In the spring of 1537, there were rumours that James was mustering troops for an invasion of England, and Henry took them so seriously that he ordered the victualling of Berwick and Carlisle. In 1541 James formally renewed the treaties of the 'Auld Alliance'. In these circumstances, it was no wonder that, when planning another war against Francis in 1542, Henry gave thought to securing his Scottish border first. He had every reason to be concerned that James would invade England as soon as the English royal army had left for Calais.[8]

Despite James's crushing defeat at Solway Moss in 1542, Henry found it impossible to subdue the Scots completely and end the French connection. His aim was not military conquest but the arrangement of an Anglo-Scottish matrimonial alliance which could bring about the dynastic union of the two realms; in this policy he was following the example of Edward I in 1290. Edward's policy had been foiled by the death of the 'Maid of Norway'; Henry's failure owed much to his bully-boy tactics which alienated the Scottish lords. In addition, he devoted insufficient political attention to the problem because of his obsession with the French campaign. After his death, the Duke of Somerset was similarly unable to overcome Scottish resistance and remove the French presence from Scotland. The issue for him, however, was not merely to secure the borders (in this he was actually very successful); he wanted to reduce Scotland to a dependency of England, initially by the use of Scottish collaborators and English garrisons, but in the long term by dynastic union. In addition to the logistical difficulties of conquering the Scots – which were considerable – it was French military aid to them that ruined Somerset's schemes.[9] There had been a trickle of French troops into Scotland immediately after the Battle of Pinkie, but French aid escalated dramatically in 1548. Six thousand men landed at Leith in June; the following July, Henry II became 'Protector' of the Scots; and in August he whisked the young Queen Mary off to France to marry the *dauphin*. Over the remainder of the year, English garrisons north of the border came under attack and one by one had to be surrendered. French intervention in Scotland had never before been so direct or extensive. The new initiative there stemmed from Henry II's ambitious dynastic policies and aggressive intentions towards England. When *dauphin*, he had developed plans to secure the union of the Scottish and French crowns by marrying Mary to his eldest son. Once king, he showed his determination to recover Boulogne and possibly take Calais too. Initially, he was prepared to bide his time, but the Battle of Pinkie forced him into immediate action. Abandonment of his 'auld' ally to his traditional enemy was unthinkable.[10]

Over the next two years, Henry II maintained his level of support to the Scots. Simultaneously, he entertained ambitious schemes of indirect involvement in Ireland. During his father's reign Ireland had seldom attracted French interest, but a group of Irish exiles, gathered at Henry's court, persuaded the king to plan a diversionary operation in

Ireland during the 1549–50 Anglo-French war. In 1549, Henry agreed to subsidize the Scottish Earl of Argyll in an attack on Ulster, and in addition the French started negotiations to provide aid to Irish malcontents in uprisings against the English. In 1550, news was heard at Dublin 'of such a hudge armye of Frenchmen to prepare t'arrive here, they be wonderfully dismayed'; but in reality, French intervention in Ireland never left the planning stage. None the less, with French attacks also mounting against Boulogne, all England's land frontiers were beleaguered and the costs of defence were astronomical.[11] Warwick's government, therefore, acknowledged defeat in the 1550 Treaty of Boulogne whereby France was left a free hand in Scotland, and Boulogne was yielded to Henry II.

During Mary I's reign the French consolidated their hold on Scotland. Mary of Guise (James V's French widow) introduced Frenchmen into her royal household and, once made regent in 1554, she appointed Frenchmen to positions of power in government. In April 1558 her daughter, Mary Queen of Scots, married the *dauphin* to whom the crown matrimonial was granted in November.[12] Despite this threat to English interests, at no time during her reign did Mary I plan any aggressive action to dislodge the French presence from her northern borders. Yet, she found herself constantly on the defensive from French aggression towards all her borders, because her marriage in 1554 to Charles V's son, Philip, had aroused fears at the French court that England would join the Habsburgs in war against France. Henry II had reacted at once to the match, dispatching men to Scotland to defend his protectorate against an invasion from the south. The following spring (1555), he also began building up his military presence at Ardres, partly for defence but also with the intention of invading Calais, were England to join the Habsburgs in a war against France. Mary's response was to assure the French of her intention to remain neutral and to try and negotiate a Franco-Spanish truce; at the same time, however, she ordered the wardens of the marches to be on their guard. Similarly, once a new war between Philip and Henry II broke out in Italy in the autumn of 1556, the French were convinced that Mary would soon aid her husband, and they began to make military preparations against England. Rumours reached the English court in late 1556 that Henry was sending more troops to Scotland and that English exiles based in France were planning to attack Calais. This time, Mary sent the Earl of Pembroke to Calais in December 1556 to reinforce the garrisons in the Pale, while assuring the French that her action was not intended as a preliminary to war.[13]

Once war broke out between France and England in June 1557, the borders were very vulnerable. Mary did not have the resources to send a large force to the north and therefore wanted to avoid open war against Scotland. On 18 July a continuation of the peace between the two realms was proclaimed at Carlisle and Dumfries, but before the end of July French troops with their Scottish allies had laid waste the English border lands and it was feared that they were bent on seizing the disputed fortress of Berwick, which was poorly fortified. The number of attackers, however, was fewer than 1000 men, and they were soon repulsed by the forces of the wardens of the marches and the northern earls. In April 1558, Sir Henry Percy launched a successful assault on the Scottish town of Langton, inflicting perhaps a hundred casualties and capturing some 400 prisoners.[14] More French troops arrived in the summer of 1558, however, and Mary's government feared that they would attack the English in Ireland as well as raid the English borders. Consequently, Mary appealed to Philip for help. At the very least she expected him to declare war on Scotland and suspend trade with her enemy, but she also looked for some naval support; Philip, though, did not oblige on any front.[15]

As soon as war was declared on the French, the governors of Calais and Guisnes, Lords Wentworth and Grey of Wilton respectively, expressed concern about the state of the defences in the Pale. Reinforcements were sent from England, but again in late December 1558 Grey complained that the three main fortresses of the Pale – Calais, Hammes and Guisnes – were inadequately supplied with men and victuals to withstand the anticipated French attack. In addition the 'hard and frosty weather', he feared, would benefit an enemy invasion, since the protective marshlands within the Pale were now frozen and could be crossed by an invading force. In his opinion, therefore, the English army would prove unable to hold onto all English territory, and he even recommended that the town of Guisnes be immediately abandoned. In response, the council ordered the dispatch of some reinforcements but a few days afterwards rescinded the command, on hearing from Wentworth that the French had designs on Hesdin rather than Calais.[16] On New Year's Day 1558, the Duke of Guise at the head of 27,000 men appeared before Calais, and on 7 January the town and castle were captured by the French. The battery of Guisnes began ten days later and the garrison capitulated on 21 January against the wishes of Grey, whose troops threatened to fling him over the walls if he did not surrender.[17] Immediately afterwards, further French invasions were feared and the government took action to secure the Channel Islands, also poorly forti-fied, and the coast of Kent. The Council, however, refused to send rein-forcements to join Philip's army for the recapture of Calais, and argued that they had neither the men nor money for such an enterprise.

The loss of Calais was not caused by treason, as the Council suspected, but was the result of misfortune (the weather), miscalculation, and low English morale. Early on during the peace negotiations at Cateau-Cam-brésis, Philip tried to negotiate its restoration, for not only was his repu-tation at stake, but also his popularity and influence within England. Even after the death of Mary in November 1558, he remained commit-ted to securing its recovery, as he was desperately anxious to retain the Habsburg alliance with England's new ruler, Elizabeth I. It soon became obvious, however, that Henry II was determined to hold on to this last piece of English territory in France, and by the beginning of February 1559 Philip knew that he could not afford a new campaign to win it back for his English ally. Aware of this situation, Elizabeth speedily signed a peace with the French, but one which left Calais in their hands.[18] Ceding the town was a humiliating start for the new regime and Elizabeth felt it keenly. The loss of England's last French possession, moreover, affected its future foreign policy in two important ways. First, as troops could not be landed easily and safely on the Continent without a beach-head on the French coast, it limited England's potential for future involvement in European wars. Second, it shifted England's southern border to the Channel, which could operate as an effective defensive moat, thereby focusing more attention on the northern frontier, England's only remaining land border, which had become correspondingly less secure. In the context of 1559, England's northern neighbour was France as much as Scotland, for in the words of Jane Dawson: 'An English bridge-head in France had been replaced by a French bridgehead in Britain', and the 'old postern gate where the Scots could create a diversion had become the front door through which a French army might march'.[19] The death of Henry II in July 1559, made England's encirclement still tighter, since his successor, Francis II, was by marriage the King of Scot-land, while his chief advisers were the powerful Guise brothers (Francis Duke of Guise and the Cardinal of Lorraine), the two uncles of his wife, and brothers to the regent, Mary of Guise (see Chart 4).

In Scotland itself, these dynastic changes helped create anxiety among the Protestant lords, calling themselves the 'Lords of the Congregation', and in 1559 they took up arms in revolt against Mary of Guise. Unsur-prisingly they turned to the Protestant ruler to the south for assistance.

Their initial pleas for military help, however, went largely unheeded by Elizabeth, though some small sums of money were delivered to them. The queen had serious reservations about supporting rebels, as well as justifiable fears concerning a confrontation with France. By the winter of 1559, however, the position of the lords was growing desperate. They had suffered some military defeats at the hands of the regent and been driven from Edinburgh, which they had earlier captured; furthermore, French reinforcements were due to arrive in response to Mary of Guise's requests for additional help. Once again the lords urged Elizabeth to give them aid. Playing on the fact that Mary Queen of Scots had handed over her crown to her husband, they presented themselves as patriots acting 'for the defence and weill' of Scotland, rather than as zealots taking up arms against their ruler on behalf of religion. Fear of extensive French intervention in Scotland forced Elizabeth's hand. As Mary of Guise was proving capable of defeating the lords without requiring further forces, Elizabeth suspected that the French were exploiting Protestant rebellion to provide a justification for building up a stronger military presence in Scotland, which could then be used as a base for an invasion of England: 'we find no small danger ensuing to our realm if the realm of Scotland should be conquered, as appeareth is meant by the men of war now in Scotland', she told her ambassador in France.[20] On 16 December 1559, therefore, she ordered her admiral to use his fleet to intercept the French and prevent them landing at Leith. Nevertheless, she remained vehemently opposed to sending an English army into Scotland to aid the Protestant lords. Winter was approaching and some of her councillors were advising her on the basis of past experience that it was easier to move into Scotland than to come out again 'with honour, or at the least without danger'.[21] Her Secretary, Sir William Cecil, on the other hand, was convinced that troops had to be sent over the border to save the Protestant lords. In this he was probably influenced as much by his religion as the question of security; some historians have also suggested that he had more ambitious plans and was considering the deposition of Mary Queen of Scots as a first stage in realizing his vision of a union of the two Protestant realms under Elizabeth.[22]

At a meeting on 24 December 1559, the council united behind a policy of war in Scotland. It recommended that a small force of about 4500 men be mustered and sent north under the command of the Duke of Norfolk. Initially, Elizabeth rejected this advice, but she retreated after Cecil threatened to resign. Caution still ruled her day, and she warned Norfolk on 29 December to follow a wait-and-see policy before crossing over the border. But although Norfolk had initially refused his command and spoken out against a land war in Scotland, he became convinced soon after his arrival at Berwick that a formal treaty should be negotiated with the Scottish lords and his troops used to expel the French already in Scotland.[23] Reluctantly Elizabeth followed his advice, and on 27 February 1560 her commissioners and the leaders of the Scottish Protestants signed the Treaty of Berwick. In late March, Lord Grey (Warden of the East and Middle Marches) was ordered across the border and joined the Scottish assault on the French garrison at Leith. None the less, Elizabeth still hoped to settle the affair 'rather by communication than by force of bloodshed' and no sooner had her troops entered Scotland than she began negotiations with the French and Mary of Guise.[24] The military operation was not a success. Grey had insufficient firepower to take Leith and his assault was repulsed on 8 May. Politically, however, the expedition was a triumph. The French agreed to England's stringent conditions at the Treaty of Edinburgh (6 July 1560), and their troops left soon afterwards. The death of Mary of Guise the previous month and civil unrest at home had left the government of Francis II with little other choice.

At one level Elizabeth's military intervention in Scotland had been the traditional English response to the problem of the 'Auld Alliance': the use of an army to secure the borders and protect England from invasion. Yet in truth, Elizabeth was following a new approach in her dealings with Scotland. Unlike her father, she treated the Scots as equals and did not seek political domination of their country; unlike Somerset, she had no desire to retain a military presence there and plant garrisons on the Scottish side of the border. This is most obviously revealed in the Treaty of Berwick. One of its terms laid down that all foreign troops would leave the realm, English as well as French, and this was echoed in the Treaty of Edinburgh. The Treaty of Berwick, moreover, envisaged long-term co-operation and reciprocal aid between the two realms. Elizabeth's protection of Scotland was to last 'during the time the marriage shall continue between the Queen of Scots and the French king, and one year after'. Furthermore, the Scots promised to help Elizabeth if the French were 'at any time hereafter' to invade England, while the Earl of Argyll (one of the Lords of the Congregation) offered 'to employ his force' against Shane O'Neill in Ulster, 'to reduce the north of Ireland to the perfect obedience of England'.[25] Jane Dawson has argued that this aspect of the treaty reflected Cecil's 'British strategy', an ideological position which had as its objective 'the creation of a united and Protestant

British Isles'.[26] It is more likely, however, that the thinking behind it was pragmatic rather than ideological. As England could not afford to keep troops in Scotland permanently and Somerset's garrisoning policy had already proved unfeasible, it was more sensible and economical to rely on Scottish co-operation to keep out the French and execute policies in England's interests. The Protestantism of the Scottish lords provided the opportunity for collaboration in the interests of both realms. Furthermore, as the Earl of Sussex, Elizabeth's deputy in Ireland, had been struggling ineffectively for nearly three years to control O'Neill, it made good sense to try another tactic which might prove inexpensive and more successful. Sussex had long bemoaned Scottish help to the Ulster chieftain and here was an opportunity for undercutting it.

Although the opportunities afforded by the Treaty of Berwick were not fully exploited or realized, the danger from Scotland diminished considerably thereafter. The 1560 Treaty of Edinburgh broke the 'Auld Alliance' and ended the French military hold on Scotland. Scottish links with France did continue until the death of Francis II in December 1560, but the Lords of the Congregation governed Mary's native land and owed only nominal allegiance to their absentee ruler. Their establishment of Protestantism in the summer of 1560 ensured that there would be no return to pro-French policies after the widowed Mary went back to rule her realm in 1561. Thus, following Elizabeth's brief but successful intervention in Scotland, power was in the hands of a strong Protestant party which was bound by ideology to its southern neighbour, and could normally be counted upon to pursue anglophile policies. This group looked to Elizabeth as their protector and a few of their number, including John Knox, even advocated a dynastic union with England. The French monarch and the Guises were usually powerless to intervene, since the civil unrest in France (which lasted until 1598) absorbed their attention and limited their potential for military action abroad.[27]

None the less, the danger from Scotland did not disappear overnight. On the contrary, for nearly thirty years after the Treaty of Berwick Elizabeth's government was beset by fears that foreign influence would return to Scotland. During Mary's period of rule, these anxieties focused around the question of her remarriage. Even in normal circumstances, the marriage of a female ruler to a foreign prince would be of considerable concern to a neighbouring power. In the case of the Scottish queen, the matter was vitally important, as a foreign ruler might promote her ambition to be named Elizabeth's successor or, worse still, claim the English throne during Elizabeth's lifetime. As a result, Elizabeth made it perfectly clear to Mary that her marriage into the Valois or Habsburg family would be considered a hostile act. When Mary wed her first cousin, the English-born Henry Stewart, Lord Darnley, in 1565, Elizabeth and her Council were no less disturbed because of the dynastic implications (see Chart 2). The amity between England and Scotland, consequently, broke down for the remainder of Mary's reign.[28] Despite the danger posed by the Scottish queen, Elizabeth greeted with dismay the news of her imprisonment and deposition in 1567. She was 'full offended' with the Scottish lords for their illegal treatment of a sovereign, and afraid that it might serve as an example to others. Indeed, her displeasure was so open and extreme that Cecil feared she would push the Anglophile lords away, with the result that 'the French may and will easily catch them, and make their present profit of them, to the damage of England'. Cecil himself wanted Elizabeth to keep Mary a prisoner in England and support the new regent, the Earl of Moray, who in his opinion 'doth acquit himself very honorably, to the advancement of Religion and Justice'.[29] Elizabeth, however, only half-listened to her minister. She accepted his advice that the strength of her reaction to the deposition might end in Mary's execution, and consequently toned down her threats of war. On the other hand, she still refused to recognize Mary's baby son, James VI, as king and tried to negotiate the restoration of Mary to the Scottish throne, though 'with some tollerable conditions to avoid perill'. The fatal flaw in this policy, at first unappreciated by Elizabeth, was that the two Scottish sides were irreconcilable; while James VI was alive, Moray refused to have Mary back on any terms whatsoever, whereas Mary's adherents expected her to be restored immediately under the tutelage of a council. By the end of 1569 a deadlock was reached. Realizing therefore that Mary's stay in England would be longer than first anticipated, Elizabeth decided to make her 'a nerer geste', transferring her from Bolton in the North to Tutbury in the Midlands. Her anger with the Scottish lords, however, could hardly be contained and for a time England's previous close relationship with the Scottish Protestants was on the brink of collapse.[30]

Even without Elizabeth's aid, Regent Moray was able to keep a tight control over Scotland, although he proved unable to crush the Marians, who continued to hold out in Dumbarton Castle. In January 1570, however, the civil war veered out of control when Moray was assassinated by one of Mary's supporters. The death of the Protestant regent was 'the worste accydent fer England that could have happened in eny feren place', bewailed the Earl of Sussex, Elizabeth's Lord Lieutenant in the

North, with considerable justification. As Scotland slipped into anarchy, the king's party suffered desertions, the Marians grew bolder, and the French king, Charles IX, threatened military intervention. Without English assistance, it appeared that Mary's Catholic and pro-French party would triumph: 'if the matter be left to them selfs, the whole wilbe shortly on that side and then no partie but one', complained Sussex again in April 1570. The Marians, moreover, were demonstrating their hostility to Elizabeth by harbouring the Northern lords who had fled into Scotland after the failure of their rebellion and had been ever since carrying out raids over the borders.[31]

Yet despite this danger, Elizabeth was averse to giving either diplomatic or military aid to the king's party. Her reluctance was partly because she still viewed its members as rebels, but mainly out of fear that the French and Spanish kings would begin retaliations against her. Nevertheless, there was a way of helping the king's party that she could justify both to herself and her neighbours. She could send her northern army into Scotland to avenge the attacks of the English rebels and their Marian friends, and to defend the frontiers from further assaults. With this her declared purpose, therefore, she ordered her troops across the border and instructed Sussex to give the king's party limited military assistance, 'in respect theyr adversaires are allso ours'.[32] Sussex stretched the queen's instructions as far as he dared. During the spring of 1570 English troops made two expeditions into Scotland. In April they captured Hume and Fast Castles; in May they joined with the king's party assembled at Edinburgh and advanced to relieve Glasgow Castle, under siege from the Marians. Cheered by this success, Sussex hoped to obtain Elizabeth's express approval for an attack on the important Marian stronghold of Dumbarton Castle. Elizabeth, however, disappointed him. Charles IX had threatened her with 'a kind of war' if she did not remove her troops from Scotland, and in response she ordered Sussex to withdraw his army and negotiate a truce between the two Scottish parties, while in England she opened up talks with Mary's representative, the Bishop of Ross, to discuss terms for a restoration.[33]

Elizabeth, however, was forced to continue as the protector of the king's party, because the Marians in Scotland spurned her offers of mediation and refused to follow her directions. Though on the defensive, they would neither come to terms with their opponents nor accept the English choice of a new regent. At the same time, they threatened to call in the French and were resuming their protection of the English rebels, who again raided the borders. Pressed by Sussex to act, Elizabeth agreed to another punitive raid into Scotland. This third expedition (August 1570) had the desired effects: the border lords submitted to Elizabeth; the rebels left the country; and the Marians agreed to a truce.[34] With the security of the Scottish king's party thereby assured, Elizabeth resumed her negotiations with the Bishop of Ross. The talks, however, dragged on inconclusively until September 1571, when Cecil uncovered details of a plot to depose Elizabeth, woven by a Florentine banker, Roberto Ridolfi, which implicated both Mary and the bishop. Immediately after this discovery, Elizabeth abandoned Mary. The negotiations for her restoration were abruptly ended, and £1000 was sent to the Marshall of Berwick for use on behalf of the king's party in the continuing civil war. In early 1572, moreover, she detached the French king from protecting his sister-in-law. During negotiations for an Anglo-French treaty she secured Charles IX's agreement that all reference to Mary should be excluded from its terms. Signed in April 1572, this Anglo-French entente (the Treaty of Blois) effectively sidelined the Scottish queen and left Elizabeth with a free hand to help her enemies in Scotland. Consequently, in the autumn of 1572 English troops joined with those of a new Scottish regent, the Earl of Morton, and captured Edinburgh Castle. This marked the end of the Scottish civil war and brought stability to that realm for the next few years.[35]

Elizabeth's relations with Regent Morton were fairly amicable but uneasy. During his ascendancy, the borders were safe and relations between the two realms were cordial, but because his control over Scotland provided her with a high degree of security, Elizabeth saw no need to subsidize him or make him her special protégé. Against the advice of her senior Secretary, Sir Francis Walsingham, therefore, she turned down Morton's requests for a defensive league and pensions for the Scottish lords.[36] In 1578, moreover, she gave him no help when his hold on power was under threat from rival Protestant lords. His enemies, she believed, would seek to retain her friendship. More importantly, in 1580 she failed to provide Morton with military or financial assistance to ward off his final downfall at the hands of James VI and his new-found favourite, Esmé Stewart Sieur d'Aubigny, who was his cousin and an associate of the Guise family. Nor would she lift more than a diplomatic finger to save Morton in 1581, when he was charged with involvement in the conspiracy to murder James's father, Lord Darnley, and executed. She was hamstrung by the fear that her intervention would offend the French king with whom she was trying during these years to negotiate a protective alliance against Spain. The alliance, she believed, had to be her priority.[37]

Over the next two years Elizabeth resisted her councillors' calls for intervention in Scottish politics. In 1582 she watched from the sidelines while a group of Protestant lords detained James VI at Ruthven Castle and banished d'Aubigny from Scotland, although English money found its way into the hands of the conspirators. Similarly, she did nothing to prevent the 1583 coup by the Earl of Arran against the Ruthven regime, even though it left James's government in the hands of a group of Marians who were hostile to England. Again and again, against the advice of her councillors, she refused to spend large sums of money to build up a pro-English party in Scotland; in her view such largesse would be a waste of her resources as the lords would not provide value for money. Instead, Elizabeth put out feelers to James himself. As early as 1583 she proposed to offer him a yearly pension and a league, but in return she expected him to follow her directions on his marriage and foreign policy. For the meantime, however, James was determined to pursue an independent course. Yet, unlike most of her councillors, Elizabeth was not particularly worried. In the first place, she was sure that the French were incapable of sending troops or even large-scale subsidies to Scotland. Second, she was fairly confident that James would be kept in check by the leverage of the succession question. In the event and against the odds, she proved to be right. Neither Henry III nor the Guises did intervene, and in 1585 James responded positively to English proposals that he enter a league with England. Another change of regime in Scotland furthered the progress of the negotiations. An English-backed coup toppled Arran, and James emerged as a more independent ruler who was prepared to reach terms with England. In March 1586 he concluded the Treaty of Berwick and became a pensioner of the Queen of England.[38] For the rest of the reign Elizabeth was at peace with her northern neighbour. Between 1586 and 1603 James received some £58,000 from the queen, and on the whole he remained loyal to his paymaster, though he pursued an independent foreign policy and was never entirely trusted in England.

As Scotland ceased to be the postern gate for an invasion of England, Ireland increasingly became a focus of foreign attention where papal, Scottish and Spanish assistance to the Gaelic lords seemed to pose a formidable threat to England's control. During the 1560s and 1570s, Irish exiles gathered at the Spanish and papal courts with the intention of securing foreign military backing for Catholic rebellions in Ireland. Their activities were well known to the English, raising fears that the Catholic powers were resolved on conquering Ireland, 'whereby heresy might be expelled and true religion planted'.[39] In reality, though, both Philip II and the pope were slow to commit themselves to intervention. Not until the militant Gregory XIII was elected pope in 1572 did the papacy develop a strategy towards Ireland, while Philip II provided assistance to Irish rebels only after Elizabeth started giving aid to the rebels against his rule in the Netherlands.

The first foreign invasion of Ireland took place in the summer of 1579 when James Fitzmaurice Fitzgerald landed at Dingle Bay in Munster with a small force in the pay of the pope (see Map 4). Although Fitzmaurice himself was soon killed in a skirmish, the invasion triggered major rebellions in Munster and Leinster led by the Desmonds and Lord Baltinglass. In 1580, a larger army of 550 regular soldiers and 800 volunteers arrived in Ireland as reinforcements, and established itself in the harbour of Smerwick. Philip II was more directly implicated in this second venture: the troops had set sail from a Spanish port and were led by Spanish officers. It was the pope, however, that most Englishmen saw behind the venture. Consequently, the English government responded vigorously; a large army besieged Smerwick and, when it surrendered, the garrison of 600 men was massacred. Inevitably, the Spanish involvement confirmed English fears about a Catholic league with Philip II at its head, and this gave further ammunition to those councillors who wanted the queen to send English troops to fight alongside the rebels in the Netherlands. The rebellions in Ireland were eventually suppressed in 1583, but their cost to the English government had been nearly £500,000 (more than five times that of the Northern Rebellion). As a result, the government looked for a cheaper solution to the security problem of Ireland, and embarked on a policy of plantation in Munster which would settle English soldiers on the confiscated rebel lands in order to keep the province under control.[40]

Unsurprisingly, during the Anglo-Spanish war of 1585–1603 the English viewed Ireland as a major security threat. Believing that the loyalty of the Catholic Irish was suspect, they feared that a Spanish army would land in Ireland and raise the country against Elizabeth's rule. As Sir Walter Raleigh observed in 1593, the Irish 'are so addicted to papistry that they are ready to join with foreign forces'. At the very least, Spanish intervention would create a law and order problem, pin down English troops needed on the Continent and drain away huge sums of money; at worse, the Spaniards might even take over all or part of the island. Though vastly exaggerated, these fears of Spanish invasion were not entirely imaginary. In 1594 Philip sent one of his captains to

Ireland to survey the coasts and harbours there, but the king soon lost interest, fully occupied as he was in Continental wars on several fronts.[41] A little later, the rebellion of Hugh O'Neill, Earl of Tyrone, caused Spain to look again at Ireland. In 1595 O'Neill wrote to the Spanish government, claiming his confederacy was for the establishment of the Catholic religion in Ireland and offering the kingdom to Philip II. The following year Spanish agents arrived in Ireland with the intention of assessing the military strength of the Irish lords and the feasibility of a Spanish landing. As a result of talks with the Spaniards, O'Neill and his allies decided to continue their confederacy. They committed themselves to an alliance with Spain and petitioned Philip to appoint the Cardinal Archduke Albert as their prince.[42] On his side, Philip offered the lords money and munitions, and authorized two armadas which set off for Ireland in 1596 and 1597. Both expeditions were unsuccessful, however, as the fleets were either wrecked or scattered by tempests on route. Over the next few years the Spaniards refrained from further active involvement, despite O'Neill's extraordinary victory in 1598 over a 4000-strong English army at the Battle of Yellow Ford. Philip III, the new Spanish king, was trying to negotiate peace with England and thus unwilling to risk another expedition. With the failure of peace talks in 1600, however, he listened to Irish plans for joint military action against Elizabeth's government, in the hope that it would drive the queen to make concessions at the negotiating table. Originally it was planned that some 6000 men should set off for Ireland to give support to O'Neill, but in the event only about 3400 landed at Kinsale in Munster, where they awaited reinforcements from Ulster. Kinsale was a poorly chosen site, and the Spaniards within it were soon sealed off by a large English army under the command of the Deputy, Lord Mountjoy. None the less, Mountjoy's troops soon found themselves on the defensive, hemmed in by the armies of the Irish chieftains who had moved south to relieve the fortress town. In the bitter winter conditions of January 1601, Mountjoy's army might well have surrendered had the Irish chieftains sat still and waited (as it was, some 6000 English soldiers died from illness and exposure). But O'Neill was persuaded by his allies to engage in battle and his army was routed. Nine days later, on 12 January 1602, the Spanish garrison surrendered. All threats to Ireland from the rebels or foreign powers were decidedly over, but the financial cost of this success was very high – close on £2,000,000, which was more than the total expenses of the war in France and the Netherlands.[43]

(ii) Dynastic Security

Throughout the late-medieval period, European rulers had interfered in England's dynastic affairs by succouring the king's rebels and supporting pretenders to the English throne. Charles, Duke of Burgundy gave Edward of York (Edward IV) money and ships to help him recover the throne from Henry VI in 1471, and in 1485 King Charles VIII of France aided the invasion of Henry Tudor (Henry VII). At one time or another, Emperor Maximilian, Charles VIII and James IV of Scotland each provided a haven for Perkin Warbeck, who claimed to be Edward IV's younger son, Richard Duke of York. Maximilian and the Archduke Philip had also taken under their protection Edward IV's nephew, Edmund de la Pole, and only handed him over to Henry VII in 1506 (see Chart 3). This foreign interference was nearly always designed for some political advantage. Charles VIII, for example, backed both Henry Tudor and Perkin Warbeck in order to neutralize the English government when he planned to incorporate Brittany into his kingdom. In all these cases the threat to the dynasty had to be taken seriously.

During the sixteenth century, the European powers continued to dabble in English domestic politics. They had plenty of opportunities for this interference; not only did members of the exiled de la Pole family continue to wander around the Continent in search of foreign aid, but in addition Henry VII's and Henry VIII's dynastic policies had greatly complicated the succession. The latter's matrimonial politics had weakened the dynastic position of his two daughters and encouraged international intervention in England's domestic affairs. As for the former, the marriage of the king's elder daughter, Margaret, to James IV had brought the Scottish Stewarts into the line of succession (see Chart 2). After 1509, James IV claimed to be heir presumptive in his wife's name, and even after his death in 1513 and the birth of Henry VIII's daughter Princess Mary in 1516, there remained the danger that the Stewart male line might challenge the claim of a female Tudor to the English throne. Later on, during Elizabeth's reign, Margaret's granddaughter, Mary Queen of Scots, claimed her place in the succession. Far from exploiting the Stewart claim to create a future dynastic union of the two Crowns, both Henry and Elizabeth refused to recognize their place in the succession. Henry dismissed as 'haughty and covetous' Margaret Tudor's suggestion that her young son should be made Prince of Wales and granted lands in England. Although Elizabeth gave signs that she considered

Mary to have the best claim to the succession, she rejected all her cousin's petitions to be named heir. Mary's religion and foreign birth made her an unwelcome candidate for most English Protestants, while Elizabeth feared that 'in assuring her of the succession we might put our present state in doubt'.[44]

Despite contemporary perceptions, the danger from Yorkist pretenders during Henry VIII's reign was hardly serious (see Chart 3). At his accession, Edmund de la Pole was languishing in the Tower under sentence of death. Admittedly, Richard de la Pole, his younger brother, was a pensioner of the King of France, but Louis XII was too preoccupied with the wars in Italy to consider military backing for an English pretender against a popular new king. Besides, until 1512 Louis hoped to keep Henry as an ally. Nor would James IV support the de la Poles, as he had previously protected Warbeck, because of his own claims to the English succession; hence in 1505 he had denounced the Duke of Guelders for harbouring Edmund and in 1513 he reminded his ally Louis XII of his own right to the English succession in the hope that the French king would not recognize his rival.[45] None the less, once Henry had decided upon war with France, the danger immediately arose that Louis would endorse Edmund and arm Richard. To meet this contingency, Henry acted swiftly. In April 1513, before setting off to France, he ordered the execution of Edmund. Henry's action was both symbolic and practical. It invoked the memory of Henry V who had marked his invasion of France with the execution of the Southampton plotters, and at the same time the removal of a pretender was a sensible precaution while the king was abroad.

Louis XII did in fact recognize Richard's title on the death of his brother, but nothing came of it. With the 1514 peace, moreover, Louis banished the pretender from France. Over the next eight years he was based in Lorraine, but there were rumours of his meetings with Francis I, who continued to offer him protection. No sooner did Henry declare war on France in 1522, than Francis made plans to send Richard with an army to invade England or Scotland. For a time this threat of a Yorkist invasion caused Henry's government considerable anxiety, but in the event Francis was too caught up with his losses in Italy and the threat to Paris to spare troops for de la Pole. All danger from Richard ended with his death on the battlefield at Pavia in 1525.[46]

For almost a decade, the Yorkist threat also seemed at an end. Until the break with Rome, the remnants of the de la Pole family caused Henry no problems, while Henry Courtenay, the grandson of Edward IV, was one of the king's closest companions. Then, in the early 1530s, Lady Margaret Pole (Edward IV's niece) came under suspicion of treason, because of her intimacy with Henry VIII's discarded queen, Catherine of Aragon. When in 1536 Margaret's younger son, Reginald, wrote a diatribe against Henry's schism and began touring foreign courts in a mission to promote a crusade against the schismatic king, the whole Pole family was viewed with deep mistrust. The Pilgrimage of Grace and Pole's new missions in 1539 sealed their fate: Both Henry Courtenay, Marquis of Exeter, and Henry Pole (Margaret's eldest son) were executed for treason; Margaret herself was imprisoned until brought to the scaffold in 1541, while her grandson and heir disappeared in the Tower (see Chart 3). As for Reginald Pole himself, he narrowly escaped the attempts of Henry's agents to capture and assassinate him.[47]

It is debatable how far Henry VIII's concern to secure his dynasty influenced his foreign policy before the break with Rome. On the one hand, Professor R. B. Wernham has suggested that both Henry's search for an imperial alliance in the early 1520s and abandonment of it in 1526 were probably consequences of his concern about the succession. In 1521 Edward Stafford, Duke of Buckingham had been accused of treason for criticizing the king and listening to prophesies that he, and not Princess Mary, would succeed Henry, and soon afterwards the king was devising plans to marry his daughter to the strongest ruler in Christendom, Charles V. Wernham and others have argued that these two events were not unconnected and that the Imperial alliance was initiated for its matrimonial clause. Consequently, after Charles repudiated the marriage contract in 1525, Henry decided to sign the Treaty of the More with Francis I.[48] On the other hand, both Professor Scarisbrick and Peter Gwyn find this interpretation unconvincing. As they point out, Henry was more concerned with his current reputation in 1522 than with the future security of his kingdom. In any event, a dynastic arrangement with Charles V was unlikely to resolve the succession issue. Matrimonial alliances included in sixteenth-century treaties were notoriously unstable, and this dynastic arrangement was particularly fragile as Mary was still a child in 1522 while Charles, aged twenty-two, was ready to marry and sire an heir.[49] Nor was Henry's decision to annul his marriage to Catherine of Aragon prompted by the failure of the Imperial matrimonial contract. Personal and domestic considerations influenced that decision. None the less, once Henry had decided to marry Anne Boleyn, his foreign policy was affected, and between 1527 and

1533 Henry steered his diplomatic efforts towards securing from the pope the annulment of his first marriage.

With hindsight it is clear that Henry VIII was wrong in his presumption that civil strife would automatically follow the accession of a female ruler. Both Mary and Elizabeth saw off challenges to their rule, and for the most part the English nobility remained loyal to the Tudor dynasty. None the less, the gender of Henry's heirs did create some problems when it came to the question of their marriage, although historians have tended to exaggerate them. As it was generally believed that a good wife would always defer to her husband, many of her English subjects initially feared that Mary I's marriage to Philip of Spain, would allow power to slip into the hands of a foreign ruler and that consequently 'strangers' would fill court positions and royal policies would be carried out in the Habsburg interest. Discontent with the match was first expressed at court and soon led to the outbreak of Wyatt's Rebellion in January 1554.[50] The marriage treaty negotiated by the Council, however, dealt with most English concerns, and Mary publicized its clauses in a proclamation of 14 January in order to allay her subjects' fears. By its terms, Philip's powers were strictly limited within the realm: he was to enjoy all Mary's titles but was denied a role in policy-making and the exercise of patronage; Mary would not be allowed to leave the country and, if she died leaving a young heir, Philip was to have little influence over the upbringing of his child. Although hostility to the marriage certainly continued, Spanish pensions won round many nobles and courtiers. Only the French were thoroughly alienated by it, with the result that Henry II's court acted as a haven for English rebels, malcontents, and even one claimant to the English throne (in the person of Thomas Stafford, the grandson of the last Duke of Buckingham). When the issue of Elizabeth's marriage was raised, many at court believed that the terms of Mary's matrimonial contract would provide adequate safeguards for the realm. Thus, despite the warnings of men such as Sir Thomas Smith and John Stubbs (both of whom wrote strong words against a foreign match), most Privy Councillors favoured a foreign consort for their queen, provided that her marriage treaty replicated that of 1554. This left Elizabeth free to seek a husband abroad: in the 1560s she entered into matrimonial negotiations with the Archduke Charles of Austria, both to provide for the succession and cement the Habsburg alliance, which was then under some strain; later she tried to secure an alliance with the French on the back of a marriage to, first, Henry Duke of Anjou (1570–1) and then his younger brother Francis Duke of Alençon (1578–81). In no way did her gender limit Elizabeth in the formation of a matrimonial policy.[51]

Ironically, not only were Henry VIII's fears concerning a female heir unfounded, but his very attempt to secure his dynasty through the annulment of his marriage to Catherine of Aragon proved counter-productive and actually weakened the Crown. In the short term it resulted in a papal excommunication and the threat of foreign invasion; over a longer period it created dynastic uncertainty, and encouraged foreign powers to meddle in English domestic affairs. In 1534 Princess Mary was declared a bastard on the grounds that her parents' marriage had been invalid, and she was only restored to the succession by an act of parliament in 1543–4. Her cause was taken up by her first cousin, Charles V, who plotted in 1535 to smuggle her out of England, and thereafter tried to mediate with Henry on her behalf. His ambassador, moreover, intrigued with the Aragonese faction that was working for the downfall of Anne Boleyn and the restoration of the princess to the succession. Charles V carried on acting as Mary's protector during the reign of Edward VI, when her continued adherence to the Mass so antagonized the Protestant regime that she was in physical danger. On the other hand, Charles was too preoccupied in 1553 with his war in Germany to offer Mary armed support when her accession was challenged by Lady Jane Grey. Indeed he counselled her to flee rather than raise her standard in defence of her throne. On the other hand, his enemy, Henry II of France, gave some help to Northumberland in order to retain his alliance with England and exclude the pro-Habsburg Mary from the throne.[52]

Like Mary, Elizabeth's claim to the succession depended on both the 1543–4 Act of Succession and Henry VIII's will, since she had been declared a bastard after Anne Boleyn's execution in 1536. Additionally, however, Henry's marriage to Elizabeth's mother was not recognized in canon law. Consequently, as far as some Catholics were concerned, her right to rule was in considerable doubt. Mary I was of course convinced of the illegality of the Boleyn marriage. She, consequently, considered repealing the Act of Succession and making her first cousin, Margaret Countess of Lennox, the heir presumptive, but she had been forced to relent in the face of opposition within the Council. King Philip too was unwilling to agree to Elizabeth's exclusion for fear that it would allow the French to claim the English throne on behalf of Mary Queen of Scots. As a result of this support, Elizabeth's accession in 1558 was smooth and unchallenged. None the less, throughout her reign the queen faced

dynastic challenges to her rule, which were usually supported by one or
other of the European rulers. Immediately after her accession, Henry II
promoted the title of Mary Queen of Scots who had married his son in
April 1558. His negotiators at Cateau-Cambrésis argued that they could
not surrender Calais to Elizabeth as it would impugn his daughter-
in-law's title to the English throne; Mary, meanwhile, publicly bore the
arms of the monarch of England. After the king's accidental death in
July 1559, Francis II acceded to the throne and Mary became Queen of
France. To the alarm of the English government, their seal bore the legend 'Francis and Mary, King and Queen of France, Scotland, England
and Ireland'.[53] With Mary's Guise uncles dominating policy at the
French court, there was, therefore, a well grounded expectation that
Francis would take military action on behalf of his wife's claim. This fear
explains Elizabeth's reaction to the build up of French troops in Scot-
land and her eventual decision to send military aid to the Lords of the
Congregation. Her anxiety about Mary's pretensions can also be seen in
clause six of the 1560 Treaty of Edinburgh, where it was agreed that the
Scottish queen would cease using the title and arms of England.

Mary, however, refused to ratify the treaty, for fear that it might pre-
judice her right to the succession. None the less, she offered to renounce
her title to the English throne during Elizabeth's lifetime in return for
official recognition of her status as heir presumptive. Elizabeth, however, would not agree. Without guarantees of her cousin's good behaviour, the danger to her security appeared immense, 'she [Mary] being a
puissant princess and so near our neighbour'. As a result, relations
between the two queens were severely strained during the early years of
Mary period of rule in Scotland. They deteriorated further once Mary
started to look for a second husband and turned her eyes towards a
Habsburg prince. Desperate to avoid this danger, Elizabeth decided to
propose her own English candidate for Mary's hand, and put forward
the name of Lord Robert Dudley, her present favourite and past suitor.
Bizarre as this scheme seemed at first, the Scots soon began to see its
advantages: it could be the means to resolve the succession problem and
preserve Anglo-Scottish amity. At negotiations held at Berwick in 1564,
therefore, both sides agreed that Elizabeth would recognize Mary's right
to the succession provided that she in exchange demonstrated goodwill
by renouncing her immediate claim and marrying the English queen's
most trusted minister. Though accepting this deal in principle, Mary
unrealistically demanded from Elizabeth that her right of succession
should be ratified in an act of parliament. Such a guarantee was beyond

Elizabeth's power to deliver. She could only make a public declaration in Mary's favour and suppress all her rivals, but for the Scottish queen this was not enough. Consequently, Mary believed that she had nothing to gain from a Dudley marriage and the match collapsed, much to the relief of Dudley himself.[54]

Mary's choice of husband fell instead on Lord Darnley, the son of Lady Margaret Lennox. News of the wedding was greeted with panic at the English court. In addition to arousing deep disquiet about the succession, some members of the Council were afraid that the marriage marked a move by Mary towards Counter-Reformation politics. Because she had secured a dispensation from the pope to marry her cousin and the wedding was marked by a nuptial Mass, some observers believed that she intended to dismantle the Protestant Church in Scotland and join an international Catholic league. The opposition of some of the Protestant lords (including Mary's half-brother, the Earl of Moray) to the marriage served to confirm these rumours. To meet this danger, Elizabeth's advisers in the north urged her to dispatch men and money to Moray, who had drifted into rebellion. Initially Elizabeth agreed and sent some money north, but she soon began to doubt the wisdom of this policy. The Spanish ambassador warned her that 'when subjects show disobedience it was very inexpedient to help them and a bad precedent for others', while his French counterpart intimated that unprovoked war against Mary might mean war against France too. Furthermore, Elizabeth had reason to fear that armed intervention might prove very costly. Her earlier expeditions abroad had taxed England's military and financial resources, and this projected campaign looked to be no less expensive, especially as it increasingly became clear that she could not count on the military help of a large Protestant party in Scotland. In contrast to the situation in late 1559, her Council shared her misgivings about intervention; though divided, it advised restraint and Cecil came out against immediate military intervention. Elizabeth was plainly relieved. Her failure to support Moray was, none the less, a humiliating climb-down and represented a diplomatic victory for Mary. The latter's power in Scotland was growing, whereas Elizabeth's credit there was diminishing. Only Mary's political incompetence, which resulted in her forced abdication, saved England from the danger of Scottish aggression to secure Mary's dynastic future.[55]

Mary's deposition and imprisonment in England did not end the threat to Elizabeth, as in their turn both the Guise family in France and Philip II of Spain took up her cause. They were not concerned, however, with the succession but in seeking to replace Elizabeth with a Catholic queen. The second and third Dukes of Guise and the Cardinal of Lorraine had always asserted their kinswoman's claim to be the legitimate Queen of England; and after 1568 they devised plots to free her from captivity, depose Elizabeth and re-establish Catholicism in England. For this reason, it was a linchpin in Elizabethan foreign policy to prevent the Guises from gaining supreme political power in France. Since the main bulwark against the Guises in France was the faction of the Huguenots, Elizabeth had a strong dynastic interest in ensuring their political survival in the French civil wars. As already seen, she had first given help to the Huguenots in 1562 when she dispatched an army under the Earl of Warwick to Normandy. [56] After Warwick's fruitless and expensive campaign, however, Elizabeth was more cautious about Continental expeditions. Consequently, she usually held back from direct military intervention in the later French civil wars, despite the many rumours of Guise plans to free Mary from imprisonment in England. None the less, she never abandoned the Huguenots and tendered them indirect aid, which took the form of loans and secret supplies of munitions. In 1568, for example, they were granted unofficial aid through an arrangement whereby the Huguenots based at La Rochelle would exchange some of their products for munitions from the English Merchant Adventurers. At the same time, moreover, Elizabeth tried to maintain a friendship with the French royal family, Catherine de Medici and her sons, in an attempt to stop them taking up Mary's cause. It was in this spirit that she signed the Treaty of Blois in 1572 and participated in the negotiations for an Anglo-French marriage alliance during the early 1570s. Only on one occasion before the outbreak of international war in the 1580s did she contemplate intervening directly in the French civil wars. In 1575 she was negotiating the dispatch of troops to assist a broad-based anti-Guise coalition which had taken up arms against the new French king, Henry III. This was, however, an act of desperation, born from the fear that the ultra-Catholic Henry would prove to be a puppet of the Guises and an agent of their Counter-Reformation policies. The danger passed when Henry was forced to come to terms with the Huguenots in 1576, fortunately before Elizabeth had committed herself to war. The threat from the Guises, however, did not abate and reached another crisis point during the mid 1580s. In 1584 Elizabeth heard the details of the Throckmorton plot in which Henry, Duke of Guise, planned to lead an invasion aimed at rescuing Mary and deposing Elizabeth. In early 1585, moreover, she learned that under the terms of the Treaty of Joinville

(December 1584) Philip II had offered protection and subsidies to the Catholic League headed by the Guises. With good reason, therefore, the English government believed that the Catholics abroad were uniting to destroy both international Protestantism and Elizabeth of England. Over the next few years it became clear that the Catholic League was gaining dominance in France and Philip II was building up an armada against England. It was against this background of a Franco-Spanish invasion scare and further plots to take her life that Elizabeth reluctantly decided upon the trial and execution of Mary in 1587.

During Mary's period of captivity, she also attracted support from Philip II. This was a new development, since the Habsburgs had stood aloof from the Scottish queen before 1568. One reason for their detachment was her close connection with France, but in addition her record as queen in Scotland had done little to endear her to either Philip or the emperor. In particular, her toleration of the Protestant Church in Scotland seemed clear evidence of a lack of commitment to the true faith. Both Philip and Ferdinand had therefore objected to the pope challenging Elizabeth's title, and displayed little enthusiasm for a matrimonial alliance with Mary. On the other hand, they had both favoured a match between Elizabeth and the Archduke Charles of Styria, which was first proposed in 1559 and then revived from 1565 until the end of 1567.[57] As Anglo-Spanish relations became more problematic, however, Philip's attitude towards Mary began to change. After the quarrel with Elizabeth over the confiscation of Spanish bullion and the imposition of a trade embargo between the two realms in 1569, Philip listened to the conspiracies of Roberto Ridolfi, who was plotting with Mary, the pope, and several English noblemen for a Catholic coup against Elizabeth. On 7 July 1571 the Spanish Council of State approved Ridolfi's plan and a week later the king ordered the Duke of Alva (his governor-general in the Netherlands) to invade England.[58] Similarly, in the early 1580s Philip was outraged with Elizabeth over her aid to the rebels in the Netherlands, and he consequently endorsed the Throckmorton conspiracy for a Guise invasion of England. Yet, in spite of Spanish support for plots against Elizabeth, Philip always remained ambivalent about Mary's suitability to be Queen of England. Not only had her marital adventures scandalized him, but he also recognized that she might prove difficult to control. In addition, were Mary to rule England, there would be problems about the succession. Her heir, James VI, was in Philip's eyes 'a confirmed heretic' who could not be trusted to convert or advance the Catholic cause. For these reasons, when first planning an armada in the mid-1580s, Philip intended to stake his own claim to the English throne rather than promote that of Mary. Genealogical charts were, consequently, concocted to prove his right through the Lancastrian line of John of Gaunt.[59] In a sense, therefore, the execution of Mary in 1587 was a blessing for Philip. Her bequest of her rights to Philip rather than to James VI further strengthened the Spanish claim. Until the end of his reign, Philip promoted the title of his daughter Isabella to the English throne.

Mary Stewart's standing as the legitimate Catholic claimant to the throne made her the figurehead for international Catholic plots throughout her period of captivity in England. Yet, though a terrifying spectre for Elizabeth's advisers, she was far less dangerous in exile within England than she had been as Queen of Scotland. At no time after 1567 did she have the wholehearted and undistracted support of any Catholic power, while from 1572 onwards Scotland was cut off from her influence. In addition, from the moment of her arrival in England, Elizabeth's government monitored her correspondence and visitors, so that the conspiracies surrounding her were discovered before they became too dangerous. There was never any chance of Mary escaping and rallying a Catholic army to her cause. Besides, after 1570, the vast majority of English Catholics remained loyal to Elizabeth.[60] None the less, the strong and well-founded belief that Philip and the Guises were conspiring with Mary and the English Catholics for the deposition or assassination of Elizabeth had an enormous impact on foreign policy.

(iii)   The Counter-Reformation Threat

The Catholic powers were slow to respond to Henry VIII's break with Rome and the introduction of Protestantism to England. Between 1533 and 1553 Habsburg–Valois rivalry over Italy kept France and Spain apart and stopped them uniting against the schismatic and heretical English monarchs. During the brief periods of truce between Francis I and Charles V, the latter was usually preoccupied with the more pressing problems of the Turkish threat or the Lutheran challenge to his empire. Besides, he was reluctant to enter a war which would dislocate the profitable trade between England and the Netherlands. For his part, Francis I had little enthusiasm for a joint crusade in the 1530s against a potential ally, and opposed unilateral action by Charles for fear that it would greatly bolster his power.[61] Before the accession of Mary I, England appeared only once to be under serious threat of a Catholic crusade, for a period of ten months between June 1538 and April 1539. Despite all Henry VIII's diplomatic efforts to keep the Catholic powers apart, a ten-year truce between the emperor and French king was signed on 18 June 1538. The following month the two monarchs met with Pope Paul III at Aigues-Mortes where they agreed to join together against the enemies of Christendom. In December the pope published his bull of excommunication against Henry VIII and one month later, in January 1539, Charles and Francis signed a pact at Toledo in which they promised not to enter into negotiations with England without the other's consent. Their hostile intentions were manifest soon afterwards, when the French ambassador was recalled from England and imperial warships began to be massed in Flemish ports. Although the threat of invasion caused some panic measures in England, the scare soon faded away. Ultimately, Francis would not work for the elimination of Henry out of fear that Princess Mary would be placed on the throne and act in the Habsburg interest. In the spring of 1539, therefore, Francis sent his ambassador back to London, while Charles dispersed his fleet. By 1540 Charles and Francis had quarrelled yet again over the future of Milan, and soon afterwards each one extended a hand of friendship towards Henry, in the hope of forging a new military alliance against the other.

In the second half of the century, the Catholic powers were similarly slow to take action against Elizabeth. Despite the provocations of her open military assistance to the Protestant factions in Scotland (1560) and France (1563), neither the Spanish king, the emperor nor the papal incumbents openly challenged her right to the throne during the 1560s. For political reasons, Philip II wanted to keep Elizabeth in power, and hoped to negotiate a Habsburg matrimonial alliance as the way towards returning the realm to the Roman Church. After 1560 the French were usually too preoccupied with their own internal conflicts to consider an aggressive foreign policy towards England. None the less, during this decade, many of Elizabeth's advisers sincerely – if mistakenly – believed in the existence of an international Catholic league formed to attack and extirpate European Protestantism. The resurgence of papal power at the Council of Trent and the Franco-Spanish meeting at Bayonne in 1565 fuelled their suspicions and anxieties. To meet the danger, some pressed Elizabeth to ally with the German Protestants while others urged her to marry the Habsburg Archduke Charles.[62] On her side, however, Elizabeth felt fairly confident that the Habsburgs would respect the principle *'cuius regio, eius religio'* (the prince would decide on the religion of his state: Catholic or Lutheran) established at the 1555 Diet of Augsburg.

Fears of a Catholic league against international Protestantism strongly influenced the English government's reaction to the arrival of the Duke of Alva in the Netherlands at the head of a huge army. Alva reached Brussels in the summer of 1567 with instructions to suppress the serious riots and political protests which had broken out in Philip II's Burgundian territories the previous year. Although economic and political grievances lay behind these disturbances, they had been accompanied by outbreaks of iconoclasm (the breaking of images) and many of the leading participants were Calvinists. As soon as he arrived in Brussels, Alva set up a special judicial court known as the 'Council of Troubles' which found guilty nearly 9000 accused of rebellion or heresy (of whom over 1000 were executed). The attitude of Elizabeth to the arrival of Alva and his suppression of the rebels was ambivalent. On the one hand, she accepted that Philip's use of force against his subjects was the legitimate action of a sovereign to restore order in his territories. On the other, she was deeply apprehensive about the presence of so large and experienced an army in the Netherlands, fearing that the king might follow up the suppression of the Calvinist rebels with military action against the French Huguenots and Protestant England. There were justifications for these anxieties. From his base in the Netherlands, Alva was intervening in the internal affairs of his neighbours; not only did his troops cross into Germany to attack rebel leaders, but, even more worrying, some of his horsemen were sent to help the French Crown in their second civil war against the Huguenots. Geography, moreover, made England particularly vulnerable to attack from the Netherlands; the deep-water harbours of Flanders and Zeeland, together with the prevailing winds, made that area an excellent springboard for an invasion of the southeast of England.[63]

Over the next few years, this sense of insecurity deepened as Elizabeth quarrelled with Philip and a serious breach developed between England and Spain. The origin of the Anglo-Spanish breach between January 1569 and 1573 lay in a number of relatively trivial disputes which deepened through inept diplomacy. These included the expulsion of the English ambassador (John Man) from Spain in early 1568, attempts of English merchants to break through the Spanish monopoly in the Indies which ended in the 'massacre' at St Juan d'Ulúa, and the affair of the Spanish treasure ships (December 1568). The latter in particular could easily have been resolved by diplomatic means, but the Spanish ambassador in England, Guzman de Spes, proved seriously incompetent and allowed his hostility towards heretics to colour his judgement. On no secure evidence, he became convinced that the queen and Cecil intended to seize the bullion on board some Spanish ships which had been forced, by bad weather and Calvinist privateers in the Channel, to take temporary refuge in English ports. Without engaging in diplomatic negotiations with the English court, he precipitously urged Alva to confiscate English ships and property in the Netherlands as a measure of reprisal.[64] The effect on Anglo-Spanish relations was devastating. An embargo was placed on all trade between England and the Spanish Empire which virtually destroyed the lucrative commerce between London and Antwerp; Philip began to give support to conspirators planning rebellion or assassination plots against Elizabeth; while Elizabeth herself entered into negotiations for a protective alliance with the French monarch, Charles IX, and a marriage with his brother, Henry Duke of Anjou.

Although the Anglo-Spanish breach was officially repaired in the Convention of Nymegen 1573, good relations were never fully restored between the two realms. Many in England were now convinced that Philip was part of an international Catholic conspiracy designed to bring down the Elizabethan regime. They rightly believed he was encouraging Catholic plots within England, but wrongly held him responsible for the papal bull of excommunication, published in 1570. For his part, Philip was justifiably angry that Elizabeth had been protecting Calvinist privateers who were attacking and looting Spanish shipping; but he mistakenly blamed her for a renewal of his troubles in the Netherlands. To his mind, she had deliberately sent out a group of privateers, known as the Sea Beggars, to attack and occupy coastal towns in Holland and Zeeland in the spring of 1572. In reality, though, Elizabeth had tried to curb the Beggars' privateering activities and forced them to leave her ports as a concessionary move towards Philip. Their capture of Brill and Flushing, which started the new rebellion against Spanish rule, was entirely unexpected and accidental. The English volunteers who began to pour into Holland and Zeeland to fight alongside the rebels, however, provided Philip with fresh evidence that England's heretical queen was stirring up sedition within his territories, while the Anglo-French Treaty of Blois seemed self-evident proof of her hostility towards Spain.

Over the next decade, some of Elizabeth's most influential councillors (notably Sir Francis Walsingham and the Earl of Leicester) argued that an English army should be sent to aid the rebels in the Netherlands in order to forestall a future Spanish invasion of England. Between 1573 and 1577 Elizabeth firmly rejected this advice and resisted the rebels' appeals for direct military aid in exchange for making her their sovereign. Not only did she dislike the principle and fear the precedent of aiding subjects against their legitimate ruler, but she also wanted to avoid open confrontation with Spain. With good reason she had little faith in an English army's effectiveness against the veteran *tercios*, and lacked confidence in the value of Holland and Zeeland as allies. Nor could she count on the French king to protect her against Spain, because Charles IX had renewed war against his Huguenot subjects in August 1572; indeed, it seemed more likely that the French would join up with Spain in military action against England. War against Spain, moreover, would risk the lucrative Anglo-Iberian trade and could well disrupt England's commercial relations with Antwerp, Hamburg and Emden. Consequently, until 1578, Elizabeth decided to present herself as neutral in the conflict. At the same time, however, she supplied the rebels with covert assistance which did not go unnoticed by Spain. Her aim was to secure a negotiated settlement between the two sides: one which would restore the Netherlands' ancient liberties and remove foreign troops from their soil. After 1578, however, Elizabeth stepped up her aid to the rebel leaders. In 1578 she subsidized the Calvinist mercenary John Casimir of the Palatinate to fight on their behalf; in 1581 she sponsored the Flanders expedition of Francis, Duke of Anjou (the French king's brother and heir); and in 1585 she signed the Treaties of Nonsuch which committed her to sending over an army to assist the Dutch provinces still in revolt. The reasons for her gradual but increasing involvement lay in the complex political and military situation that developed in the Netherlands during these years, and in the fear of Spanish policy and power which pervaded government circles.

In 1576 those provinces of the Netherlands which had previously remained loyal to Philip II came out in rebellion, after unpaid Spanish troops had mutinied and sacked their towns, most notably Aalst and Antwerp. All the provinces came together and agreed upon the Pacification of Ghent (1576), which called for the expulsion of all foreign troops from the Netherlands, the suspension of the heresy laws, and maintenance of the religious *status quo* in all provinces. The Pacification was accepted by Don John, the new Spanish governor-general, in the

Perpetual Edict (1577), and a cease-fire was negotiated. Elizabeth thoroughly approved the terms of the Pacification and promised to send an army to the Netherlands if Don John repudiated it. The fragile peace, however, soon collapsed and in January 1578 the Spaniards won a resounding victory over the States-General's army at the Battle of Gembloux. It now seemed that Philip II would be able to impose an unconditional military settlement on his rebels. In desperation, the States-General repeated their offer to grant the English queen sovereignty in return for her military assistance. At the same time, Catholic deputies of the States-General turned to the French Duke of Anjou for aid. These unexpected events placed Elizabeth in a serious predicament. She believed that a Spanish victory over the rebels would endanger her realm, yet at the same time she could not allow Anjou to assist them for fear that the French would gain influence or territory in Flanders as a reward. In the famous words of the Earl of Sussex: 'the case wylbe harde bothe with the Queen and with Ingland yf ether the Frenche possesse or the Spanyardes tyranyse in the Low Contryes'. Despite her earlier promise, she did not want to send troops herself, wary of the financial cost and fearful about the consequences of a direct contest with Spain. The Council, moreover, was giving her conflicting advice; whereas Walsingham and Leicester counselled active military intervention in the Netherlands, others recommended caution, while the Earl of Sussex put forward a plan that she marry the Duke of Anjou (although he was her junior by nearly twenty years) as a preliminary to an Anglo-French league.[65]

Initially, Elizabeth responded to the problem by sending out English volunteers and using Casimir as her subsidized mercenary in a holding operation. In the summer of 1578, however, she came to favour the option of the Anjou marriage. To her mind, a French matrimonial alliance would solve a number of urgent problems. First, it might frighten Philip into making peace in the Netherlands on her terms. Second, it would allow her to control the ambitious Duke of Anjou and prevent Flanders falling into the hands of the French Crown. Finally, it would end her diplomatic isolation, for Henry III would be unlikely to join with Spain and attempt 'eny thing that may be prejudicyall to her Majestie and her husband his brother'.[66] As the matrimonial negotiations proceeded, however, Elizabeth's objectives began to change, and from the early autumn of 1580 until late 1581 she tried to secure a French offensive military alliance against Spain. This shift in policy was the result of both an intensification of 'the Catholic threat' and a dramatic growth in

Spanish power during these years. In terms of the former, 1580 was a particular *annus horribilis* for the English government: Pope Gregory XIII's re-issue of the bull of excommunication against Elizabeth, the arrival of his agents, the Jesuits, in England, James VI of Scotland's dependency on the 'very Catholic' d'Aubigny, and the landing of Spanish troops in the West of Ireland, all exposed England's vulnerability to the forces of the Counter-Reformation. As for Spanish power, by 1581 it was looking invincible. In that year Philip was recognized as King of Portugal after a successful military campaign to assert his claim to the throne. He thereby acquired a formidable fleet which could be used in an invasion of England and a vast colonial empire which could help finance it. On the Netherlands front, rebel unity had fractured, and the new governor-general, Alexander Farnese, Prince of Parma, had successfully reached terms with the Walloon provinces of the south in 1579. In 1581 he looked poised to reconquer the north. It was no wonder then that Elizabeth believed that French help was needed to combat Spanish power. Without it, England's military endeavours against Spain would be futile and dangerous. Elizabeth's plan was that a French army could take on the Spaniards in Flanders, while her fleet would give underhand aid to Dom António (a pretender to the Portuguese throne) and attack Spanish shipping.[67]

Marriage with Anjou proved impossible because of political opposition to it within England on religious grounds; but without the marriage Henry III refused to agree to any alliance with Elizabeth. In these circumstances Elizabeth appeared to have little other choice than to act as Anjou's unofficial paymaster in the Netherlands. Isolated as she was, she still hoped to avoid open war with Spain, but she recognized that without foreign aid the Dutch rebels would be totally defeated or forced into an unconditional surrender. Few English observers doubted that a Spanish invasion of England would follow the suppression of the rebellion. Consequently, in December 1581 Elizabeth agreed to provide Anjou with two 'loans' of £30,000 each, and in February 1582 she sent him to the Netherlands as her protégé accompanied by a delegation of forty or so English nobility and gentlemen. In the event, Anjou's military involvement in the Netherlands neither helped the rebels nor removed the long-term threat to England. He quarrelled with the States-General, won no victory over Parma, and lost half his troops in an abortive attempt to capture Antwerp (which was not even held by the Spaniards). Meanwhile, Parma was capturing a string of towns in Flanders and Brabant.

The death of Anjou in June 1584 hardly constituted a serious setback to the rebel cause. None the less, the States-General, backed by Elizabeth, at once solicited Henry III to take his brother's place as their protector. On the other hand, the assassination of the rebel leader, William of Orange, in July was potentially disastrous for the States-General, and Elizabeth feared that without foreign aid the rebels would become so demoralized that they would make peace with Spain on Philip's terms. To avert this danger, she immediately instructed her ambassador in France to urge Henry to 'impeach the Spanish power' and take the Netherlands under his protection, but the king's answers were 'cold' and unforthcoming. Apparently, Henry suspected that Elizabeth would be glad to see the Kings of France and Spain at war 'whereby both their horns might be the better pared...and her own estate the more assured'. Furthermore, challenged by the Catholic League at home, Henry was in no position to help Calvinist rebels abroad.[68]

By November 1584 Elizabeth could wait for Henry III no longer, and she offered to open discussions with the States-General about the terms for her aid. With her Council divided, however, over whether or not to commit English troops to the Netherlands, she avoided making any final decision until March 1585, when it became absolutely certain that Henry would not act as their protector. Any remaining opposition to military intervention faded away in June with the news of two actions recently taken by Philip II: first his conclusion of the Treaty of Joinville with the Catholic League, and second his seizure of English shipping and merchandise in Spain, which was thought (quite wrongly) to be for the purpose of building up an armada to attack England. Consequently, the Council united behind a policy of war and Elizabeth signed the Treaties of Nonsuch with the States-General in August and September 1585. The terms met both her security and financial needs; she agreed to provide the Dutch with £126,000 a year until the end of the war as payment for an English force of 6400 foot-soldiers and 1000 cavalry. In return, they would deliver to her some cautionary towns as insurance that they would not enter 'any reconciliation' with Philip II without her consent, and as a guarantee for the repayment of her expenses at the end of the war. In order to avoid 'long, bloody wars' with Philip she refused to accept sovereignty of the Netherlands and would only agree to take the Dutch under her protection.[69].

In September 1585 Elizabeth at last took military action against Spain: she appointed the Earl of Leicester general of her troops in the Netherlands, and authorized Sir Francis Drake to rescue the English ships detained in Spain and to plunder Spanish shipping in the Caribbean. Both these decisions were taken with the intention of forcing Philip II to sit down at the negotiating table with the rebels and sign a peace on the basis of the Pacification of Ghent. Elizabeth still hoped to avoid a full-scale Anglo-Spanish war. Hence, she opened up at least five simultaneous sets of peace negotiations with Spain between 1585 and 1588, and worked herself into a fury when Leicester accepted the governor-generalship of the Netherlands. But Elizabeth's military operations, limited though they were, had entirely the opposite effect to her intention. Philip could hardly overlook the provocation of English raids on his coasts, plunder of his ships, and succour to his rebels. Consequently, in December 1585 he decided to embark on a grand enterprise against England. The Spanish Armada, which eventually set sail in 1588, was designed to protect his territories and reputation; but it was also a religious crusade 'to subdue that kingdom to the authority of the church of Rome'. During the weeks before the campaign, the king ordered a programme of prayer to demonstrate his holy zeal and guarantee his victory. English Protestants, too, saw the coming conflict as a war of religion; in describing the Armada, one piece of propaganda declared: 'It is the Romish Antichrist which hath blown the trumpet of that cruel sedition.' Its 'defeat' was therefore viewed in England as an act of providence, and Leicester was not alone in thinking that 'God hath also fought myghtely for her Majestie.'[70] Divine favour, however, did not end the danger from Philip. The Spanish fleet soon recovered from its losses, and fresh armadas were launched in 1596, 1597 and 1599, which were all the more menacing with Ireland in rebellion. The Spanish army continued to press hard on the forces of the States-General until the loss of Groningen to the Dutch in 1594 relieved the pressure on the north. In the late 1580s, moreover, a new danger emerged: France looked set to fall to the Catholic League which was allied to Spain. This dangerous development was the result of the factional and religious conflicts within France which had come to the fore on the death of Anjou.

The death of the last Valois prince left Henry of Navarre, the Huguenot leader, as heir to the French throne, a circumstance which was intolerable to most of the Catholic world. The Guises immediately revived the Catholic League, secured the protection of Philip and took up arms in order to exclude Navarre from the throne. For the rest of his reign, Henry III wavered in his allegiances: in 1585 he signed the Treaty of Nemours with the League, but until 1587 he left its generals to do the fighting against Navarre. That summer he raised his own army against the Huguenots, but in October 1588 he organized the assassinations of Henry, Duke of Guise and Louis, Cardinal of Guise, and in April 1589 he signed a truce with Navarre. After Henry III's own assassination in August 1589, Philip decided to intervene directly on behalf of the League. Navarre was proving to be a very able commander who had wrested all the major towns in Normandy from the League. With Paris under threat, Philip ordered Parma in 1590 to lead an army to relieve the French capital. Spanish troops also arrived in Brittany, and in 1594 threatened to establish a fortified base around Brest.

Well before this Spanish intervention, Elizabeth was alarmed at the turn of events in France. As early as the spring of 1585 she had tried to rally the Lutheran princes of Germany and the King of Denmark behind Navarre, but without success. In 1586 she lent Navarre £30,000 to raise an army of 9000 German mercenaries under Duke Casimir, money which was wasted in a fruitless campaign in France in 1587.[71] Casimir's failure led Elizabeth to confine herself to less expensive methods of support. She allowed Navarre's agents to recruit men and buy arms in London, while her diplomats tried to wean Henry III from the League. On Navarre's accession to the throne, however, she succumbed to his urgent pleas for assistance. The danger of the League securing military control over Normandy and its Channel ports was too great to ignore. Consequently, she ordered 4000 men under Lord Willoughby to act as reinforcements in Navarre's Normandy campaign. The success of Willoughby's four-month campaign encouraged Elizabeth to send further forces once Spanish troops were employed in France. Once again she preferred to concentrate her efforts on keeping the Channel ports out of hostile hands. Two further expeditions set off for France in 1591: 4000 men under the Earl of Essex to Normandy to help Henry IV besiege Rouen, and 3000 under Sir John Norris to Brittany to expel the Spanish garrison there. Neither campaign achieved its purpose; indeed, Essex's Rouen campaign was so disastrous that Elizabeth balked at sending more troops to France. On the other hand, in 1594, English troops under Norris captured the castle of Morlaix and the Spanish fort at Crozon which commanded Brest harbour in Brittany. In fact, by the mid-1590s, the threat to England from Continental Europe was pretty much at an end. Henry IV had gained a firmer hold over his kingdom after his conversion to Catholicism in 1593, and the danger of a Spanish or Guise dominance over France consequently evaporated. A year later the Spanish threat to the United Provinces also diminished. This meant that Elizabeth could afford to disengage from expensive continental warfare and concentrate instead on privateering raids at sea and on suppressing O'Neil's confederacy in Ireland, which was increasingly attracting Spanish intervention. In early 1595, Elizabeth not only began the withdrawal of troops from France, but also commenced negotiations with the States-General for the repayment of her loans. Only after the Spaniards had captured Calais in 1596 did the queen again commit troops to France but, after its recapture the following year, she immediately recalled them.[72]

With hindsight, it is clear that Elizabeth's ministers overestimated the danger from Philip II and the Guises, who had too many problems of their own to consider a crusade against England. None the less, the government's fears appeared well-founded at the time, especially given the alarmist reports of its spies, agents and ambassadors abroad. It is also easy to criticize Elizabeth's responses to the security crises she faced. On the one hand she has been accused of doing 'too little too late' to help the Dutch rebels and French Huguenots. On the other hand, the very measures she took to protect herself from Spain encouraged the invasions and plots she most feared. In addition, a long line of historians have argued that her policies were too often hesitant, ill thought out, and simply *ad hoc* responses to particular crises.[73] It is true that some of her decisions were quixotic, such as the Anjou matrimonial scheme. Other decisions, however, were cautious but sensible (certainly far more so than the interventionist policies advocated by Leicester and Walsingham); they also had clear objectives in view. Elizabeth aimed to check the power of the Guises without alienating the French king by supporting Calvinist rebels too openly. She intended to avoid war against Spain while demonstrating to Philip that she was a ruler whose interests he could not afford to ignore. These were difficult tightropes to walk, and it is not surprising that she sometimes stumbled or hesitated before taking steps, especially as she was so often buffeted by events outside her control. Furthermore, Elizabeth was operating in a world where many of the assumptions on which England's foreign policy had traditionally rested no longer held true. No more were there two leviathans in Europe, each seeking an alliance with England against the other. The Habsburg alliance looked far less valuable after the disruption to the Antwerp staple in 1569 and its collapse in the mid-1570s. Confessional conflict was now dominating the political life of France and the Netherlands. In these new, unfamiliar circumstances, it was inevitably going to take time for a coherent and successful policy to evolve. Given these difficulties, Elizabeth did remarkably well in her foreign policy: she assisted the survival of the Calvinists in France and the Netherlands; she avoided bankrupting the Crown in over-ambitious exploits; and she emerged triumphant, if rather battered, from the eventual international conflict.

4

RELIGION

The previous chapter demonstrated how the Reformation had a major impact on foreign policy by transforming the nature and extent of England's problems relating to security and defence. This chapter looks at some different aspects of the changes brought about by the Reformation. The first section traces through Anglo-papal relations in order to explain and assess the impact of the pope's hostility to England's schismatic rulers. In the second section, England's relations with other Protestant states are explored, with the emphasis on the moves to forge a league with the German Lutherans. The last section on the 'godly cause' assesses the influence of religious ideology on these and other foreign-policy decisions. This is by no means a straightforward task. Monarchs and their ministers frequently employed the rhetoric of religious aspirations, and it is practically impossible to reach firm conclusions about the sincerity of their protestations. At almost every point, moreover, secular interests and religious motives coincided: how then does an historian give weight to one set of considerations rather than the other? Perhaps the most that can be said is that ideology has usually been neglected in books on English foreign policy, and religious rhetoric has been too often dismissed as a cloak designed to conceal secular concerns. The belief here is that rhetoric can reveal a particular mind-set which helps shape reactions and responses to events; it should, therefore, be taken into account rather than cynically put to one side. Furthermore, in my view, too little regard has been given to Elizabeth's sympathy for her co-religionists abroad. In this section, I hope to readjust the balance.

(i) Anglo-Papal Relations

Henry VIII's relations with the papacy before 1529 gave no hint of his future anti-papal policies and break with Rome. On the contrary, during these years Henry liked to present himself as a defender of the Church by attacking schismatics, offering to take up arms against Islam, and penning a response to the heresies of Luther. In addition, Henry VIII and the popes generally worked towards a common end in international affairs: a league against France from 1511 to 1514; European peace in 1518; an alliance with Charles V in 1522; and a coalition designed to remove imperial power from Italy from 1526 to 1529. A. J. Pollard has argued that this pro-papal policy was the work of Thomas Wolsey who wished 'to hitch England to the Holy See' in order to advance his career within the Church. The reality, however, was different. First, it is doubtful whether Wolsey had any designs on the papal tiara, as he neglected to build up a party of supporters in Rome, a first priority for anyone with aspirations in that direction. Furthermore, he only reluctantly put himself forward for election in 1521 and 1523, when pressed to do so by the king. But even had Wolsey held ambitions to be pope, he was in no position to control policy; Henry kept a close eye on all the diplomatic exchanges between courts and played the key role in decision-making. In any event, a close examination of Anglo-papal relations before 1529 reveals that the harmony between England and Rome was often a mirage. In the words of Professor Scarisbrick: 'England and Rome were frequently out of step, sometimes seriously so; and when there was an identity of purpose, the identity was often accidental.'[1]

When Henry VIII took the throne, Pope Julius II was Louis XII's ally in the League of Cambrai against Venice, and initially gave no heed to the English king's calls for an offensive coalition against France. Soon afterwards, however, Julius settled his dispute with Venice and decided to turn his energies towards removing the French military presence from Central Italy. Consequently, in August 1510 papal and Venetian troops assaulted French bases at Genoa and Ferrara. As Louis responded to this papal attack by summoning a General Council of the Church to meet at Pisa, Julius declared the French king a schismatic, formed a Holy League against him, and treated the European war that followed in 1512 as a crusade. This course of events worked greatly to the advantage of Henry VIII, a member of the league. He was now able to fulfil his ambitions and enter a war against France backed by the pope, who promised to invest him and his heirs with the 'name, glory and authority of the king of France', once he proved victorious in battle. Additionally, papal support helped break down clerical opposition to the war at home; it was hard for Archbishop Warham and Dean John Colet (both of whom had given sermons in 1512 attacking wars between Christians and extolling the virtues of peace) to continue in their stand against a war which was sanctioned by Rome: Finally, the papal alliance gave Henry the upper hand in his dealings with James IV of Scotland. The latter had hoped to appeal to Julius as the arbiter of the 1502 treaty against the 'unprovoked attacks' of Henry VIII, but he inevitably found little recourse there. On the contrary, Leo X (who was elected pope in March 1513) ordered the Scottish king to keep the peace with England or else risk ecclesiastical censure. Although this had no practical effect on James, Henry had the moral advantage which increased his confidence.[2]

After 1514, however, Henry's relationship with Leo X (1513–23) proved to be more problematic. Leo was less bellicose than his predecessor and consequently out of sympathy with Henry's attempts between 1514 and 1518 to build another coalition against France. Later on, moreover, when the two rulers appeared to be co-operating closely, they were usually working independently and pulling in different directions. Thus, their joint venture in 1518 to further international peace masked divergent motives: whereas Leo wanted concord between the European states as a preliminary to a crusade against the Turks, Henry's interest lay in his own self-promotion as a major figure in international affairs. Not surprisingly, therefore, tensions soon developed in the Anglo-papal negotiations for peace. Henry's refusal to admit the papal envoy, Cardinal Campeggio, to England unless Wolsey was elevated in the Church to become a *legate a latere* (a papal legate with the fullest powers) was an early indication of things to come. Once Campeggio had arrived at court, the king allowed Wolsey to upstage his co-legate at every turn, paid only lip-service to the idea of a crusade, and transformed the papal peace initiative into the Treaty of London which was designed to enhance his own standing in Europe.[3] Again, three years afterwards, Leo's granting of the style *Defensor Fidei* (Defender of the Faith) to the English king appeared to denote a warm Anglo-papal relationship yet, in truth, it was a hard-won and grudging concession. For six years Henry had been badgering the pope to bestow on him a title to rival those held by the Kings of France and Spain. At last when it was granted to reward Henry for his literary defence of the Church against Luther, Leo denied him the style for his heirs (limiting it to the king personally), and made the wording very simple without the flourish of '*Gloriosus*' (most glorious) or '*Fidelissimus*' (most faithful). Political relations in the same year show a similar underlying tension. Although the Anglo-Imperial treaty of 1521 followed closely on the heels of the treaty between Leo and Charles V, they were negotiated separately and the interests of the emperor's two allies did not coincide. Leo wanted a warfront to be opened in Italy immediately, whereas Henry and Wolsey wished to postpone the war for at least another year and had little direct interest in ousting Francis from Milan.[4]

After Leo's death, England and the papacy continued to tread a superficially similar path in foreign policy until 1529. On his election the new pope, Clement VII (1523–34), had hoped to bring an end to the war that was turning Italy into a permanent battlefield. At about the same time Henry began to withdraw from the war for financial reasons, and put out feelers for a negotiated peace with France. After 1525, both men switched to support military moves against the emperor, yet once again their motives differed. After Pavia, Clement VII was alarmed at the build-up of imperial power in Italy and wanted to prevent any one ruler from dominating the peninsula. On the other hand, Henry had no interest at all in the balance of power and was merely affronted that he personally had been unable to benefit from Charles's victory. His dislike of imperial hegemony in Europe was because he feared that it would leave him with no role in international affairs and exclude him from any future peace-treaty between France and the Empire.

Clearly, Henry's decision in late 1526 to divorce his wife, Catherine of Aragon, revolutionized Anglo-papal relations. At first, however, this was not obvious. Henry needed the pope's consent to the annulment of his marriage and hoped at the outset to secure it by diplomacy. But, after the sack of Rome by imperial troops in May 1527, Clement was a virtual prisoner of Charles V, Catherine's nephew, who would not tolerate Henry's repudiation of his aunt. At first, while the pope was held in actual captivity, Henry planned to bypass him by establishing a papacy in exile at Avignon; his idea was that Clement would delegate his pontifical authority to Wolsey who could then pronounce the marriage annulled. No-one in Rome, however, would co-operate with this scheme; besides, the escape of the pope to Orvieto in December rendered it obsolete. Though now physically liberated, Clement was still not a free agent but dependent on the goodwill of the emperor for the recovery of the Papal States. Clearly then, Henry's dynastic politics as well as his concern to play a leading role in international affairs led him towards the same conclusion: Charles V had to be driven out of Italy. This the king attempted to do by subsidizing Francis I and the League of Cognac. In the meantime, however, he sent embassy after embassy to the Curia to persuade Clement to issue a decretal commission which would allow the divorce case to be heard by Wolsey, as papal legate, in England without a right of appeal to Rome. Each delegation, however, returned home with unsatisfactory documentation – a worthless dispensation, useless general commissions, and a 'pollicitation' (a promise never to revoke a decretal commission) full of loopholes. In all these negotiations Clement VII proved himself adept at prevarication and evasion; through his skilful diplomacy he was successful in avoiding taking precipitate action which would alienate either Henry or Charles. Henry, on the other hand, was paying the penalty for having previously neglected to build up an English party at Rome, a deficiency which forced him into a long-distance and woefully amateurish diplomacy. All might not have been lost had the French managed to defeat the armies of Charles V, but in June 1529 the Comte de Saint-Pol suffered an irreversible defeat at the hands of the Imperialists at the Battle of Landriano. Political realist that he was, Clement had no choice but to follow the will of Charles. Consequently, in July 1529 he remitted to Rome the annulment case which had been heard in the Blackfriars legatine court, and in August he signed the Treaty of Cambrai which ended French military efforts in Italy.[5] In these circumstances, Henry could not hope for a favourable verdict when the case was heard at Rome.

Over the next four years Henry gradually proceeded towards a policy of direct confrontation with the pope. After Wolsey's fall from power (October 1529), his case for the annulment moved away from the previous conciliatory approach which had focused on the defects in the original papal dispensation allowing him to marry Catherine; now it came to centre on an outright denial of the papal right of dispensation. Henry also rejected the pope's authority to hear his court case in Rome and ordered his agents to find legal and historical evidence for this position.[6] Clement VII took his time before responding to these provocations. Although he did not dare to act against Charles V's wishes, he hoped to avoid antagonizing Henry and was therefore quite content to postpone reaching a decision on the divorce for as long as possible. Henry's assertion of imperial kingship and flagrant marriage to Anne Boleyn in 1533, however, could not be ignored; as a result, in July 1533 Clement drew up a bull of excommunication against the king. None the less, it was not promulgated until 1539, but sat gathering dust while the pope tried to persuade the secular rulers of Europe to commit themselves to implement it by declaring war on the schismatic Henry. Before 1538 this proved impossible. Not only did Franco-Imperial hostilities from April 1536 until June 1538 prevent united action, but the two Catholic rulers would not make separate moves against the English king. Francis I was Henry's ally in the early 1530s and protected him so forcefully that Clement feared that 'not only England but France would be divided from the Church' if the bull were published. On his side, Charles V was loath to execute the bull partly because he feared that Henry might retaliate by harming Catherine of Aragon and her daughter. Self-interest, however, also influenced the emperor, for he was concerned about the economic damage to the Netherlands if he broke off relations with England. When at last Paul III (1534–49) did obtain French and Spanish agreement to mount a crusade against England, their commitment was very short-lived. Both rulers were soon distracted by other interests: their rivalry over Milan, the Lutheran princes, and the forces of Islam. This state of affairs continued after Henry's death. In addition, Edward VI was protected by his status as a minor; the precedent of the pope deposing a legitimate child-monarch was a prospect too dangerous for the European sovereigns to allow. Consequently, despite their strained relations with Protector Somerset's government, both Henry II and Charles V persuaded Paul to hold back from issuing a bull of excommunication against the young king.[7]

It was to be expected that Anglo-papal diplomatic relations would run smoothly after Mary I's accession, and indeed for two years all went well. On the domestic front Julius III endorsed the Spanish marriage, and agreed that Englishmen could keep their lands which had formerly belonged to the Church, thereby facilitating the reconciliation to Rome. Furthermore, sharing Mary's desire for a European peace, he entrusted Cardinal Pole with the task of mediating between the French and Habsburgs, and during 1554 England and the papacy worked together to promote a peace conference which opened at Marcq.[8] In 1555, however, all changed with the election of the cardinal, Gian Pietro Caraffa, as Paul IV (1555–9). Thanks to his fanatical anti-Habsburg feelings and uncompromising pro-French policies, Mary found herself caught in the fallout of Italian politics and drawn into an unwanted conflict with the papacy. In 1556 Paul denounced her father-in-law, Charles V, as a heretic and schismatic; shortly afterwards the Spanish viceroy in Naples invaded the Papal States, and a French army set out towards Italy. Although Mary tried to keep out of the ensuing war, the pope tarred her with the same brush as her husband. He condemned her as 'the wife of a schismatic' accused her of giving financial aid to her husband, and threatened to use his spiritual powers in retaliation against her.[9] On 9 April 1557 he revoked Pole's legatine commission and summoned him back to Rome to answer 'certain charges' of the Inquisition. Pole had protested against the war, and possibly his strong words encouraged Paul to take action against a man he had long distrusted on theological grounds. As Mary refused to allow her archbishop's departure or the admission of a new legate into England, her relations with the pope deteriorated further. Even after Paul made peace with Philip, he remained in dispute with Mary and refused to deal with any paper work relating to England, leaving as a result her nominated bishops unconsecrated. Mary therefore died in communion with Rome but in conflict with the pope.[10]

Expectations that the 'all French' Paul IV would immediately excommunicate Elizabeth and pronounce Mary Queen of Scots the legitimate queen of England were soon confounded. Paul was persuaded against instant excommunication by Philip II who argued that a Catholic marriage for Elizabeth was imminent and would be the better way to win England back to Rome.[11] The new pope, Pius IV (1559–65), needed no persuasion to follow the path of negotiation rather than confrontation. In May 1560, he dispatched a papal envoy to England with a conciliatory message for the queen. Philip, however, feared that the nuncio would be denied entry and the pope provoked into reprisals, and so he had him detained in Brussels and sent back to Rome. A year later Pius tried again and dispatched his nuncio, Abbot Martinengo, to England with a letter inviting Elizabeth to send representatives to the papal Council of Trent which he had just summoned. At the English court, Robert Dudley tried to use his influence to secure admission for the envoy and acceptance of the invitation, in the hope that this pro-Catholic intervention would encourage Philip to look favourably upon his plan to marry the queen. Cecil, however, was fervently opposed to both a Dudley match and any accommodation with the papacy. For a brief time, Elizabeth was on the brink of permitting Martinengo to enter the realm, provided that his title was 'the ambassador of the bishop of Rome' and not 'papal nuncio'. Cecil, however, foiled the papal design; he successfully whipped up an anti-papal scare, and took the lead in the Privy Council to deny entry to Martinengo. In this climate of anti-Catholic fervour Elizabeth could do no other than refuse to send a representative to Trent. She rejected the invitation on the grounds that the council had been called solely by the pope and would only give a voice to 'such as be already sworn to the maintenance of the Pope's Authority'.[12] With this evidence before him of Elizabeth's intransigence, Pius wanted to issue a bull of excommunication and deposition at the Council of Trent but both Philip II and

Emperor Ferdinand dissuaded him and refused to recognize Mary Queen of Scots' title to the English throne. Pius, therefore, resorted again to negotiations, and tried to use contacts at Elizabeth's court to move her towards a policy of returning to Rome. His informants were so encouraging about future prospects that six months before his death Pius publicly announced his expectation that Elizabeth would marry an orthodox husband and restore 'true religion' in her realm.[13]

Pius V's (1565–72) signing of *Regnans in Excelsis* which excommunicated and deposed Elizabeth was a unilateral act taken in February 1570 with no reference to the Catholic powers. He was not expecting a foreign crusade to follow the bull but hoping that its publication would encourage English Catholics to join the Northern Rebellion, which had erupted the previous October. In fact, the rebels had already been defeated and its leaders taken flight. The Catholic monarchs were dismayed by Pius's pronouncement and inclined to ignore it: 'This is very bad', noted Philip privately, while Maximilian declared himself 'discontented' with the bull and used 'sharp words' against the pope. Charles IX of France publicly disregarded the bull by asking Elizabeth to be the godmother of his infant daughter, much to the disgust of the papal nuncio in France who refused to attend the ceremony.[14] Over the next decade, successive popes tried to implement the bull by mobilizing Philip II, stirring up rebels in Catholic Ireland, and encouraging plots against Elizabeth. Aware of these activities, most Englishmen saw the pope rather than Philip of Spain as Elizabeth's main enemy during the 1570s and 1580s. Even the Armada was seen as the pope's work; Philip was thought to be merely 'deputy therein to the Pope'.[15]

It was not until the 1580s that Philip could be persuaded to use military force against Elizabeth. By that time the pope was Sixtus V (1585–92) who was suspicious of the king's ambitions and irritated by his 'usurpation' of the rights of the Church. His support for the Spanish Armada was therefore rather half-hearted; he agreed to the proclamation of a jubilee 'to help the success' of the venture but would not issue a papal indulgence for those who took part.[16] The failure of this and later armadas dissipated any lingering hopes of the conversion of England by force. Some Catholics both at home and abroad, therefore, began to think that the pope should work for the more limited objective of obtaining religious toleration for English Catholics by negotiating directly with Elizabeth: 'what might not your Holiness do, with the aid of the most Christian King towards obtaining consolation for the English Catholics', urged Thomas Bluet in Rome. Clement VIII (1592–1605), however, felt unable to recognize formally that heresy was permanently embedded in England, while Elizabeth firmly dismissed the idea of toleration in a proclamation of 1602 which rejected 'such a course, as would not only disturb the peace of the church, but bring this our state into confusion'.[17]

The Reformation obviously transformed Anglo-papal relations; it converted the pope from a close ally in the early sixteenth-century to a relentless enemy by the end. The impact on foreign policy of this revolution has not always been appreciated. As far as Elizabethans were concerned, their belief that the pope was at the centre of a holy league against international Protestantism coloured their views on policy, fuelled their paranoia, and did much to create a nationalism which was closely allied to Protestantism. While their suspicions were entirely warranted, their anxieties were unjustified. Although the papacy retained sufficient moral authority and financial resources to act as a focus of intrigue against Protestant England, individual popes could not command the active support of secular rulers nor co-ordinate Catholic policy against Elizabeth.

(ii)   Reformation Diplomacy: Germany and the Baltic

As a result of the Reformation, new contacts were established with the Protestant princes and cities of North Germany and Scandinavia. Prior to the break with Rome, there had been commercial links with the Hanseatic cities of the Baltic; but marts were set up, for the first time, in north-German Lutheran ports during Elizabeth's reign, when relations with the Catholic rulers of the Netherlands became more troubled (see Chapter 5). In addition, both Henry VIII and Elizabeth saw advantages in developing political and religious connections with the Lutheran princes of Germany. Attempts to make a formal alliance failed in both cases, but considerable diplomatic activity was directed towards them which brought England into much closer communication with the states of Northern Europe.

The first attempts at opening up relations between England and the German Protestants were inauspicious. The initiative came from the newly formed League of Schmalkalden (an association of German Lutheran princes united in defence of their faith), which sent an ambassador to England in February 1531 to explore the possibility of

allying with Henry against the pope and emperor. On his side, Henry
saw a value in encouraging the Germans 'to maynteyne all their just
quarrells' against Charles V, but at that time the king was not interested
in entering a Protestant league since he hoped to avoid an irretrievable
rupture with the pope. After the break from Rome in 1533, however,
Henry's attitude towards the Lutherans changed. Although he was disappointed that most of their theologians had disagreed with his arguments for the divorce, he felt in need of the Lutheran princes' assistance
against the pope. In the summer of 1533 and in early 1534, therefore,
ambassadors were sent to Germany to seek 'thair advyse and assistens'
and to co-ordinate calls for a General Council of the Church. The timing
of this embassy was unfortunate, however, for the princes were too preoccupied with German matters to take up the English proposal. Meanwhile, Henry was becoming unwisely entangled in Baltic politics. In
1534 the Hanseatic city of Lübeck approved Henry's divorce and sent
a delegation to England to negotiate an offensive league against the
pope. The ambassadors arrived with theologians who held long talks
with their English counterparts on matters of doctrine, but without
reaching any agreement. On the political front they were more successful, since Henry and Thomas Cromwell could see commercial and political benefits from establishing a foothold in North Germany.
Inexperienced in the realities of Baltic politics, they became allied to the
city, then under the direction of its radical Protestant mayor, Jürgen
Wullenwever, who was rashly waging war against both Sweden and
Denmark. Although the war was doomed from the start, Henry unwisely
offered Wullenwever a loan and made preparations to send three warships to the Baltic. He was forced to retreat a year later, after the Wullenwever faction was overthrown and the new Lübeck councillors sued for
peace, but it took two more years for him to mend his fences with the
King of Denmark.[18]

Undeterred by these failures, Cromwell planned to investigate again
the opportunities for joining a Protestant league against the pope and
emperor. Initially he persuaded the king to enter into political and religious negotiations with the Schmalkaldic League as part of a general
drive to find new allies. In 1535 an embassy left for Germany and at the
same time ambassadors were sent to France, Scotland and Poland. The
overture to the League, however, soon came to be more than a search
for political allies; both Cromwell and Henry were also interested in
finding out more about the theology of the Augsburg Confession (the
confession of faith adopted by the League). Having dismantled many of

the structures and beliefs of the Roman Catholic Church, the king was looking to establish a statement of faith in England to take its place, and hoped that consultations with German theologians would provide some guidance; for this reason he also instructed his ambassadors to persuade Philip Melanchthon (the Lutheran theologian with a reputation for moderation) to come over to England. The English mission, however, was not a success. The Lutheran princes, led by the Duke of Saxony, would not consider any kind of political alliance unless Henry first sub-scribed to the Augsburg Confession, nor would the duke allow Melanch-thon's departure for England. Furthermore, the theological discussions which were held in Wittenberg during early 1536 revealed significant disagreements over four principal areas of doctrine: private masses, com-munion in both kinds, priestly marriage and monastic vows. Although Henry was prepared to debate these issues further, the German princes had no intention of making any concessions, nor of revising the Augsburg Confession to suit the King of England. They were, moreover, horrified by the news of Anne Boleyn's execution and broke off the talks, though promising to send a return embassy to England sometime in the future.

It was the pope's summons of a general council to be held at Mantua that prompted the Schmalkaldic princes to keep their promise, for they wanted to negotiate a common Anglo-German response to this threat. During the stay of the return embassy in the summer of 1538, however, it became clear that the outstanding theological differences could not be settled as the preliminary to a political accord. Henry had deliberately included a majority of religious conservatives among the English negoti-ators, and they refused to compromise on the key areas of dispute. Furthermore, the king himself intervened personally to dismiss the Lutheran position on clerical celibacy, communion in both kinds and private masses.[19] Yet, it was just at this time that Henry most needed a Protestant alliance, for a Catholic coalition was beginning to line up against England. Consequently, in June 1538 Cromwell opened talks with the German ambassadors about the feasibility of a matrimonial alli-ance and, a little later, suggested a match between Henry and Anne, the sister of William, Duke of Cleves. Henry, too, tried to keep negotiations for a political alliance alive. In early 1539, he sent an envoy to the lead-ing Lutheran princes to test out their attitude towards a Cleves marriage and to ask 'what they will do for his Grace in case he be invaded for the cause of the faith...and what contribution and aid they would for a reciproque ask'. The responses of Saxony and Hesse, however, were so cool that Henry was at last convinced that the alliance project was at an end. He bitterly complained of the princes' 'oversight and slackness in showing [such lack of] gratuity to him'. Enraged with the German Lutherans and isolated in the face of a Catholic attack, he decided to reverse his previous experiments on religion. In June 1539 he signed the Act of Six Articles as a gesture designed to show the Catholic powers that his orthodoxy was unimpeachable, thereby removing any pretext for an invasion.[20]

Despite this unwelcome turn of events, Cromwell went ahead with the negotiations for the Cleves marriage. He remained committed to the idea of a pan-Protestant league and believed that it might be advanced by this means. Duke William's political credentials suited Cromwell for he was both anti-Habsburg and the brother-in-law of the Duke of Saxony. As he was also conservative in religion, despite his schism from Rome, the matrimonial project was also acceptable to Henry who saw it as another device to end his isolation in Europe. The marriage, however, was ill-fated. Not only did Henry find Anne so unattractive that he was unable to consummate it, but the political benefits from the Cleves connection were illusory. Far from shielding Henry from the emperor, William was too weak to prevent an imperial attack on his own territories. Furthermore, it soon became evident that the rapprochement between Charles V and Francis I would not last long and that the danger to Henry's security was over. Consequently, by the summer of 1540 Anne was dispensable and her marriage to Henry was annulled in July, only six months after it had been contracted. By that time Cromwell had been brought to the scaffold. Henry could not forgive his minister for exposing him to such a humiliating experience and for failing to rescue him from the marriage more speedily; he was therefore more than ready to listen to Cromwell's enemies who were plotting his downfall.[21]

Cromwell's death left Henry without a foreign policy. The ministers who replaced him were divided over what future policy to follow, with Stephen Gardiner favouring an alliance with the emperor and the Duke of Norfolk preferring one with France. For the next two years Henry kept his options open, sending out signals to both Charles V and Francis I of his readiness to sign a treaty if the terms were right. The German Protestants were excluded from his considerations until 1545 when he hoped to bring them into an alliance against France after the emperor had pulled out of the war. Yet even after the Treaty of the Campe had been signed with France in 1546, Henry continued to show interest in a

Lutheran alliance and one of the last foreign representatives he received came from the Schmalkaldic League.[22]

At the beginning of Edward VI's reign it was the Lutheran princes who needed an English alliance as Charles V was mobilizing his forces against the leading princes of the Schmalkaldic League. In March 1547 an embassy arrived from Saxony requesting 'summe good summe of money', and Somerset's government promised that, if the Protestants survived through the summer, a loan of 50,000 crowns would be provided. Only a month later, however, they capitulated to Charles V at the Battle of Mühlberg. As a result, Protestant theologians from south Germany (whose theology tended towards the Swiss Reformed Church) took up refuge in England. This exodus was directly encouraged by the government who sent a mission to Strasbourg to invite Martin Bucer, Peter Martyr and Bernardino Ochino to England. Their influence on Edwardian politicians and divines – and consequently on English religious history – was immense.[23] Despite this sympathy to the Protestant cause, Somerset tried to obtain the emperor's goodwill, and in 1549 sent Paget to Brussels to renew the imperial alliance and negotiate a marriage for Princess Mary with the Catholic *Infante* of Portugal.[24] After Somerset's fall from power, the Council continued its efforts to avoid a rupture with Charles, and consequently remained neutral when the Lutheran princes re-opened the war in Germany. In any event, since the princes had made a military alliance with France, the English government was suspicious of their motives. In October 1551 a delegation from the Schmalkaldic League arrived at court to ask for financial aid 'in caus of relligion', but Northumberland first requested that they specify their religious objectives, 'lest when warre shold be made for other querelles they should say it were religion'. Eventually, the Council turned down the requests for money from both the German princes and their French allies.[25]

Elizabeth's accession was greeted positively by the Lutheran princes of Germany and Scandinavia, and within the first year of her reign the queen received marriage proposals from Duke John William of Saxony-Weimar, Adolphus, Duke of Holstein and Eric XIV of Sweden. Although there was little support in the Privy Council for any of these matches, there was general recognition that Elizabeth would benefit from close relations with fellow Protestant rulers abroad; the Germans could supply her with much-needed mercenaries for her war in Scotland as well as outlets for her goods, were Philip II to close access to the Netherlands. Cecil, however, was thinking beyond commercial links and wanted political co-operation as well. Elizabeth gave her backing to his initiatives. Thus, they sent an envoy to Germany in late 1561 to discuss a response to the papal invitation to the Council of Trent, and urged that a common answer be sent to Rome, 'so as consydering both their cause in that point is but one, their aunswer and dealing may be also one'. At the same time, Elizabeth promised to give consideration to discussions for the creation of a Protestant league; and in 1562 Henry Knollys was dispatched to Speyer and Heidelburg 'to sollicite the Princes Protestants bothe to ayd the Prince of Condé, and to consider how the common cawse of relligion might be defended against any common confederacy of the enemy'. The German princes, however, had no interest in an alliance with England. At a meeting at Naumburg, they did not even consider Elizabeth's proposal for a united front against the pope. A year later, Philip of Hesse and Frederick of the Palatinate turned down Elizabeth's offer of a league, claiming that their existing defensive arrangements provided them with adequate protection from the Catholic powers. None the less, they did agree to send soldiers to Condé. On the other hand, John Frederick of Saxony not only expressed hostility to a league, but declared his intention to keep the peace with the King of France.[26]

During the 1560s religious controversies over the Lord's Supper broke the fragile unity of the German Protestants. Both sides wanted to enlist Elizabeth for their side. The Lutheran princes urged her to subscribe to the Confession of Augsburg, but they increasingly lost confidence in her after hearing the many reports of Calvinist influence within England. On the other hand, Frederick Elector of the Palatinate thought in terms of a political alliance. In 1563 he had adopted Calvinism which, unlike Lutheranism, was not recognized in the 1555 Peace of Augsburg; he therefore felt isolated within Germany and vulnerable to an attack from the Catholics. Furthermore, he favoured a militant anti-Catholic policy, and in 1567 he allowed his son, John Casimir, to lead an army into France to help the Huguenots, a decision which alienated the emperor and the Duke of Saxony as well as the Kings of France and Spain. In early 1568, therefore, he sent his envoy Immanuelo Tremellius on a diplomatic mission to England to request financial aid and propose a defensive league. Elizabeth, however, offered no more than polite interest in the elector's schemes since she had no wish to become embroiled in confessional conflicts within Europe or risk the wrath of the Habsburg princes. After the rupture with Spain in January 1569, her attitude changed. An alliance with Protestant Germany then looked more attractive on both defensive and commercial grounds. It would rescue England from its dangerous diplomatic isolation, provide protection for the newly established staple in Hamburg, and ease access to the markets of the Baltic. With these considerations in mind, Elizabeth sent Henry Killigrew to Erfurt in 1569 to propose a formal alliance which would embrace the Scandinavian kingdoms as well as the Germans. The German Lutherans, however, were highly suspicious of Elizabeth. They branded her a Zwinglian or Calvinist, and Augustus of Saxony for one refused to ally with her unless she subscribed to the Augsburg Confession. They also distrusted her motives in seeking an alliance, justifiably believing that she was only interested in obtaining support against Spain. The alliance proposal was therefore not looked on with favour. In the end, it was rejected because most of the princes opposed confrontational politics with the Catholic powers and preferred a 'moderate and interconfessional policy' with the Austrian Habsburgs.[27]

The idea of a pan-Protestant league did not die at Erfurt and it was resurrected whenever the danger from the Catholic powers seemed most acute. In the spring of 1577, for example, Elizabeth responded to the crisis in the Netherlands by sending envoys to John Casimir of the Palatinate and William of Hesse to see if they could arrange a German Protestant league 'against the Pope and his adherents'. The German Lutherans, however, were threatening to denounce all Protestants who refused to adhere to the Augsburg Confession, so no security could be found from that quarter. Rather than act alone, Elizabeth decided to proceed by employing John Casimir as her mercenary in the Netherlands.[28] Again, in 1584 as news reached England of a Catholic league to suppress international Protestantism, Elizabeth tried to construct a pan-Protestant coalition encompassing the King of Denmark, the Hanseatic towns, as well as the German Lutheran princes (Brunswick, Hesse, Saxony, Brandenburg). Her plan was for joint action to foil the Catholics in France and the Netherlands. She wanted the Hanse to cease supplying Spain and France with corn and provisions, and the princes to contribute forces to help Henry of Navarre. She also appealed for their financial aid to the Protestant Archbishop of Cologne who had been driven into exile in 1583, so that he could divert part of the Spanish army and thereby relieve the Netherlands. The German Lutherans were, however, unwilling to follow her lead; religious differences with the Calvinist Huguenots and fears that any help to Navarre would provoke a hostile reaction from the emperor stayed their hand. The King of Denmark refused to move without them. Once again, therefore,

English attempts to construct a league collapsed and Elizabeth was forced to fall back on the offers of help from the unreliable John Casimir of the Palatine.[29]

Most of the responsibility for the failure of the attempts to build-up a pan-Protestant league during Elizabeth's reign should be placed at the door of the Germans. The confessional strife amongst the German states and the conservatism of Saxony repeatedly prevented its formation. None the less, a major handicap in Elizabeth's relationship with the German and Scandinavian powers was England's inadequate diplomatic representation in the area. Like her predecessors, Elizabeth employed only one resident agent in Germany and relied otherwise on unofficial sources of information and contact. Consequently the queen and her ministers demonstrated at times an astounding lack of understanding about German and Baltic politics. They tended to treat the German Protestants as a single group, and were insensitive to the political rivalries and religious differences that divided them. The queen's diplomatic efforts were littered with mistakes, as when she unnecessarily offended the Elector of Saxony in 1585 by not giving him the deference he felt due to him as the senior Lutheran prince. Similarly, Elizabeth fared badly in Scandinavia because of inexperience and inadequate contacts there; according to E. I. Kouri, 'the English were outwitted there by the French with their superior understanding of the area'. In addition, suspicions of Elizabeth's intentions had grown within Germany as a result of her merchants' commercial penetration of the Baltic region. It was, therefore, not a lack of English will that prevented the formation of a pan-Protestant league, but the negative attitude of the German princes together with inadequate English diplomacy.

(iii)   The 'Godly Cause'

Most historians today would agree that Thomas Cromwell's promotion of a Protestant foreign policy had an ideological as well as a political dimension. His interest in the Protestant cause, however, was anglocentric rather than internationalist. Cromwell's aim was to draw England nearer to the Lutheran princes in order to develop theological contacts which might encourage the king to advance towards evangelism. For a short time it seemed that he might be successful, since articles drawn up by the English and German theologians at Wittenberg in 1536 were fed into the first five of the Ten Articles published in England the same year.[30] Ultimately, however, Henry discarded Cromwell's evangelical programme, and in 1539 he preferred to play the conservative card in order to secure his readmission into the club of European monarchs.

When looking at Edward VI's reign, however, there is more debate about the influence of religious ideology on foreign policy, particularly that of Protector Somerset towards Scotland. Taking up his pen most convincingly to tear apart an earlier idealistic assessment of Somerset's character and policies, Michael Bush argued in the 1970s that the Protector was motivated solely by considerations of honour and security in his wars against Scotland. In his opinion, Somerset's religious utterances and propaganda were simply the velvet glove to disguise the iron fist threatening to crush the Scots: 'Whilst prepared to proselytise in order to increase the allegiance of the Scots, Somerset probably did not attach much importance to this approach or value its feasibility very highly...evangelism was a marginal detail of his general Scottish policy', claimed Professor Bush.[31] Today, however, several historians think otherwise. Jenny Wormold, for example, believes that Somerset saw himself 'as releasing Scottish Protestants from Catholic bondage' and the Battle of Pinkie as a religious crusade. In a similar vein, Roger Mason has argued that 'an intense commitment to the reformed faith' energized Somerset's imperialist policy towards Scotland. Both these historians and others have demonstrated that English propaganda towards Scotland expressed the ideology of a Protestant unionism, which all historians should take seriously. In proclamations and five unionist tracts, Edwardian Englishmen promised to advance the 'glorie of God and his worde', and 'to make of one Isle one realme in love, amitie, concorde, peace and charitie'. The use of military action against the Scots, moreover, did not necessarily expose the insincerity of these sentiments, as Bush had asserted, since force could be justified in religious terms. If the Scots would not accept the manifest will of God to cast out popery and unify the British Isles by the peaceful marriage of Edward VI and Mary, then, according to English Protestants, they deserved conquest: 'you will not have peace, you will not have aliaunce, you will not have concorde, and conquest commeth upon you whether you will or no' declared *An Epistle...to...the Inhabitauntes of Scotland*, thought to have been written by Somerset himself. It seems unlikely that Somerset's government employed this rhetoric as a cynical device to win over the Scots, if only because the Protestants in Scotland were still a small minority. The Protector either believed in this ideology himself or else was sending out these messages to justify his military action to his Protestant political allies within England. His exact motives have to remain obscure, but it is noteworthy that his invasion was accompanied with an assault on the Catholic Church in Lowland Scotland, as the English troops burned, wrecked and looted parish kirks, monasteries and priories.[32] It also seems that Somerset's Protestant rhetoric was not without effect. In Scotland most of the lords who collaborated with England were 'the godlie that loife the said mariage and unioune'; for them Edwardian England was identified with the Protestant cause. A little later on, they came to see Elizabethan England in the same light, and in the early years of her reign they worked for a Protestant union of the two realms. Within England, the Protestant unionist ideology permeated Somerset's circle. According to Jane Dawson, its longer-term influence was also great, moulding the outlook and affecting the later policies of men like William Cecil: 'Cecil's experiences in the 1540s when he had served Protector Somerset', she claimed, 'provided him with the ideological dimension of his strategy' in the early 1560s, a strategy of creating a united and Protestant British Isles.[33]

During the next decade and thereafter, a religious dimension to Elizabethan foreign policy is usually associated with the ideology of 'political puritanism', which counted amongst its spokesmen the councillors, Leicester, Walsingham and the Earl of Essex. The ideology has been defined by Simon Adams as 'the advocacy of assistance to the Church abroad, rather than rapprochement with the Catholic powers or *Realpolitik*, as the guide for English policy'. Its promoters believed that England had obligations to defend the Reformed Churches abroad and a duty to take up the armed struggle against the Antichrist. As Dr Thomas Wilson (Elizabeth's Secretary 1577–81) explained, the first principle in foreign policy should be the 'glorie of God and his rightuousness to bee faithfullie settled everywhere'; this could only be achieved, he thought, by following a policy whereby 'those abrode who are faithful, and of the same religion that we professe, myght be united to us, and we to them'.[34] Wilson and his colleagues on the Council, therefore, urged Elizabeth to intervene directly on the Protestant side in the European wars of religion in order to protect their persecuted brethren and defeat the forces of the Antichrist. In the late 1570s and 1580s they recommended that Elizabeth enter a Protestant league rather than sign a defensive treaty with Catholic France against Spain, although the latter seemed to be the stronger and more effective ally. Once war had broken out in 1585, advocates of 'political puritanism' wanted it to be fought for religious rather than secular ends. Thus they argued for an extensive land war which would defeat the Catholic League in France and throw the Spaniards out of the southern Netherlands, and for the establishment of permanent naval bases on the Continent from which Spanish shipping could be attacked. All in all, they wanted the Antichrist to be not merely bloodied but totally overcome. They consequently opposed the more limited and secular objectives of the Cecils.[35]

Despite his Protestantism, William Cecil is not associated with 'political puritanism', because he tended to advocate more cautious policies towards France and Spain than either Leicester or Walsingham. Yet historians are now beginning to recognize that Cecil held a similar Protestant world-view which influenced his approach to foreign policy. He too saw international politics through the prism of providentialism and apocalyptic thought – as a struggle of the true religion against the Antichrist – and felt a strong sense of solidarity with England's co-religionists abroad. His comments on international affairs often employed the rhetoric of 'political puritanism' even if the practical policies he advocated were usually far more circumspect. It was Cecil who wrote to Admiral Coligny in 1563 that he 'holds no difference between nation and nation, but that they are all of one city and country, bound to join together for the defence of themselves against anti-Christians of whatsoever country they may be'. After the Massacre of St Bartholomew, it was Cecil who commented: 'I see the Devil is suffered by the Almighty God for our sins to be strong in following the persecution of Christ's members' and later on criticized the Valois royal family for governing France 'by bloody meanes. . . to extinct the trew profession of Christ's Gospell'. Again in 1579, Cecil argued for a Protestant league 'to defend themselves against only the Pope's tyrannous, bloody and poysoning persequtors'.[36] It was this similarity of outlook that allowed Cecil to work with Leicester and Walsingham in the 1570s despite specific disagreements about policy: military intervention in the Netherlands; the Anjou matrimonial scheme of 1578–81 and the confiscation of treasure seized by Francis Drake. It was this perspective that allowed Cecil to believe in the conspiracy theories surrounding a Catholic league and to advocate the formation of a Protestant counter-alliance.

What about Elizabeth herself? Conventional wisdom, of course, states that she had little or no sympathy with the Calvinists abroad and 'constantly frustrated' the interventionist policies recommended by her ministers on behalf of the Protestant cause.[37] It is certainly true that Elizabeth had no intention of taking up the sword against the Catholics on ideological grounds. She was no biblical Deborah determined to uproot idolatry in foreign lands, whatever her propagandists might say. On the contrary, she was prepared to live in a Europe where two Christian faiths co-existed, and was firmly committed to the principle *cuius regio eius religio* (the ruler of a state would determine its religion) as laid down in the 1555 Peace of Augsburg, though she would have liked it extended informally to include the Calvinist rulers. She also believed in the principle: one state, one religion. Consequently she would no more demand that her fellow Catholic rulers should recognize and tolerate Protestantism than she would listen to their requests that she grant freedom of worship to her Catholic subjects. Thus, before 1577, she did not even put pressure on Philip II to grant freedom of worship to his Protestant subjects in the Netherlands. She merely urged him to reach a settlement which would restore to the provinces their ancient liberties, suspend the inquisition and thereby allow liberty of conscience. After 1577, however, she exhorted him to respect the terms of the Pacification of Ghent which had been agreed by his governor-general Don John in the Perpetual Edict. Her ideal solution to the Netherlands' crisis, even after 1585, was for the North to be given home rule and religious toleration but to remain under the ultimate sovereignty of Spain. As far as France was concerned, she expected its monarchs to respect the edicts of toleration which they had freely granted to their Protestant subjects. Consequently, whenever possible, Elizabeth tried to use diplomatic means to secure toleration for the Huguenots. After the massacre of the Protestants at Vassy in 1562, she offered to mediate between the French royal family and the Huguenots and seek a peace to stop 'these extremities'. After the more devastating Massacre of St Bartholomew, Elizabeth protested strongly to the French ambassador. When the French army looked set to capture the Huguenot stronghold of La Rochelle in 1573, she again offered to mediate between the two sides, and also used the diplomatic lever of her marriage negotiations with the Duke of Alençon to press the king to lift the siege and make terms with his Protestant subjects. Later on, after Henry IV converted to Catholicism, she was anxious to prevent a new persecution of the Reformed Church, and sent Sir Robert Sidney to France in late 1593 with a formal message requesting the king 'to show all the favour that he could to them of the Religion'. Sidney was also told to deliver an oral warning that were Henry not to grant the Huguenots religious freedom and political protection, 'She could not forsake them now nor suffer the cause to want assistance.'[38]

Elizabeth had serious doubts, however, about giving military support to those of her co-religionists who had taken up arms against their legitimate sovereign. Rebellion was anathema to her, and on many well-documented occasions she publicly stated her opposition to 'proceedings of subjects against their rulers'. At one time or another, she openly criticized Protestant leaders – Henry of Brederode, William of Orange and the Prince of Condé – for rebelling against their respective sovereigns.[39] Security concerns also restrained her from backing their causes. It was for this reason that she would not dispatch an army to the Huguenot stronghold of La Rochelle in 1572 or 1573, despite the urgent pleas from the Calvinists who had survived the St Bartholomew Massacre. After the experience of the Newhaven expedition she had serious doubts about the effectiveness of any English military effort in France. At the same time, she feared reprisals from the Catholic powers, who might well take action against her, were she to be seen helping heretics abroad. Similarly, the French king might be persuaded by the Guises to invade England or Scotland on behalf of Mary Stewart if she gave military aid to subjects in rebellion. Yet, despite all her reservations, Elizabeth did not passively watch the extermination of her fellow Protestants – and it is hard to believe that the reasons for her intervention were entirely political. Not only did she apply diplomatic pressure whenever possible on their behalf, but she also gave them unofficial practical help. She allowed England and the Channel Islands to become the home for religious refugees from both France and the Netherlands; and she turned a blind eye when their churches in England became recruiting ground for volunteers to fight against the Catholics abroad. From the early 1570s onwards she refused to comply with the Spaniards' demand that she order the withdrawal of English volunteers and mercenaries from the Netherlands, nor would she stop the dispatch of future soldiers. On the other hand, the Council banned Englishmen from joining the Spanish king's army as mercenaries. Active help to her co-religionists at La Rochelle was also provided both in 1570 and 1573, when the queen was willing for her ministers to arrange the shipment of money, munitions and provisions for the town's defence. Eventually, of course, Elizabeth sent armies to the rebel cause in both France and the Netherlands. In both cases the aid was limited in scope and largely prompted by concerns about national security. None the less, even when the Spaniards had been driven out of Northern France and the danger to the Channel ports had been lifted, Elizabeth did not abandon her Protestant allies. As far as the Huguenots were concerned, she was satisfied when Henry IV met their demands, first in an edict of toleration in 1594 and then in the 1598 Edict of Nantes. As for the United Provinces, despite her many bitter disagreements with them about money and military tactics, she refused to abandon the States-General and make a separate peace with Spain. Although she did not initiate any major offensive action against Spain after 1598, English troops were left in the States-General's service until her death.[40]

5

COMMERCE

Sixteenth-century English monarchs ignored economic considerations in their foreign policy at their peril. Royal income from customs dues depended on the buoyancy of overseas trade, while merchants also helped in the financing of wars by offering or arranging loans. In addition, the political support of London merchants strengthened the position of a royal dynasty, as had been clearly demonstrated during the Wars of the Roses. Finally, a healthy manufacturing base and strong export market encouraged domestic peace by staving off riots led by the unemployed. Henry VII fully appreciated these points, and his foreign policy was usually directed towards encouraging foreign trade and securing advantages for English merchants. Henry VIII, on the other hand, gave less thought to commercial considerations in his foreign policy. Perhaps this was because his other sources of income were growing at a time when the yield from customs was static, even declining in real terms. Perhaps too, negotiations for commercial treaties seemed dreary in comparison to the finding of political allies and planning of Continental wars. It was the disruption to trade at Antwerp and in the Mediterranean, together with the Crown's financial difficulties, that revived governmental interest in the customs and commerce. The Duke of Northumberland and Mary I took the first important steps towards encouraging new trade routes and eroding the privileges of the Hanseatic merchants who were the main rivals of the London Merchant Adventurers. Elizabeth followed their lead, and continued to give diplomatic and political support to London merchants. Unlike them, however, she also encouraged ambitious commercial projects to break into the Iberian monopolies over newly discovered lands in Africa and the Indies; her motives were both financial (a desire for profit) and political (to make a stand against Philip II); yet at no time did she share the imperial dreams of many of her advisers. The effect of the diversification of trade on England's economy has sometimes been exaggerated, since England's traditional European markets continued to dominate the Elizabethan export trade. Its effect, however, on foreign policy was considerable, as England's commercial expansion exacerbated tensions in Anglo-Spanish relations and opened up a new rift with the Hanseatic League and Scandinavian powers.

(i)   Antwerp Trade

During the last quarter of the fifteenth century the English cloth trade grew rapidly and by 1500 it had become the most important and profitable area of English commerce. Under Henry VIII it continued to expand, with customs figures suggesting that there was an increase of over 100 per cent in the export of woollen cloth between 1505 and 1544. A slump followed in 1551, but it was only temporary and woollen cloth exports soon settled down to a steady level under Elizabeth. In 1565 they accounted for 78 per cent of all exports. Until the late 1560s, almost the entire trade was centred on the London–Antwerp axis. Undyed and undressed woollen cloth produced in England was exported from London to Antwerp where it was exchanged for a variety of foreign goods including alum, hemp, iron and wines. The trade was largely in the hands of the Merchant Adventurers Company which depended on the Crown to enforce its monopoly and restrict interlopers. In return the Crown benefited from the customs duty on the cloth, and increasingly came to rely on the Company to provide it with some essential political and financial services. Its governor carried out the duties of an ambassador at the Habsburg court in Brussels, representing English interests there and providing information for ministers at home. In addition, from at least the early 1540s, its representatives raised foreign loans for the English monarch at Antwerp, while after 1543 the Company provided surety for the Crown's foreign borrowing. In the late 1540s, the Merchant Adventurers helped Sir Thomas Gresham in his task of propping up the rate of exchange at the *bourse* in Antwerp to facilitate the repayment of the foreign debt. For all these reasons, the Crown needed to look after the interests of the Merchant Adventurers.[1]

During Henry VIII's reign there was only one major disruption to this profitable trade. It occurred between 1527 and 1528, when Henry was allied to France against Charles V. In May 1527, Wolsey stopped the English cloth fleet from selling its wares at the great international fairs in Brabant in the expectation that Antwerp would be so severely damaged by the boycott that its leading citizens would petition the regent, Margaret of Austria, and the emperor to agree to Henry's demands in a peace settlement. After all, similar action taken by Henry VII had proved effective in squeezing political and economic concessions from Maximilian and his son Philip in 1505. At the same time, Wolsey hoped to avoid dislocation to English commerce and manufacturing by establishing Calais as an alternative mart town. Wolsey's tactic, however, misfired. First, English exporters found Calais unsuitable for their needs, and consequently transported their cloth overland to Antwerp, which raised their costs and pushed up prices. Second, the regent and emperor were furious at the English act of commercial aggression and did not hesitate to initiate their own economic reprisals after Henry declared war on Spain in January 1528. In February, Margaret arrested English merchants in Antwerp, seized their goods, and brought the cloth trade to a halt. While the Antwerp economy could survive the temporary loss of trade, the stoppage wrought havoc in England. The lay-offs in the cloth industry created unrest, and major riots were only just avoided when the government ordered clothiers to continue employing their outworkers in the manufacture of cloth. London merchants were threatened with a loss of privileges, even a spell in the Tower, if they did not purchase cloth which they would be unable to export. This situation could not go on indefinitely, and Wolsey was soon forced to negotiate a truce with the regent. The cardinal's unpopularity with the London merchants, so evident in the parliament of 1529, owed much to his disregard of their interests during the previous two years.[2] During this domestic crisis of 1528, therefore, England's over-dependence on the lucrative Anglo-Burgundian trade was plain for all to see. Since it was a dependence that could limit freedom of action in both foreign and ecclesiastical policy, Henry VIII and Thomas Cromwell were keen to escape it and find direct markets for English cloth elsewhere. It was mainly for this reason that they tried to develop links with some of the Lutheran Hanse towns (see Map 5) and became embroiled in the Lübeck fiasco (see p. 89). Their tentative search for new markets and a new staple, however, made little or no progress and the domination of the Antwerp mart continued unchecked throughout the reign.

The economic – as opposed to political – dangers of relying so heavily on a single outlet for English cloth became apparent in the mid-Tudor years. In the early 1550s, there was a glut of cloth on the Antwerp market and English traders found difficulty in selling their goods there. The government responded in ways which were to have significance for the future. As will be seen in the next section, both Northumberland and Mary began the process of seeking more distant markets for English cloth. Additionally, pressed by the Merchant Adventurers, the Council under Northumberland suspended the privileges of the Hanse (an association of North German trading cities with shared commercial interests); it banned them from purchasing English cloth in England and imposed on them the same import and export duties as were being paid by other alien merchants. The aim was to give English merchants a larger share of the remaining export trade. This attack on the Hanse had long been wanted by the Merchant Adventurers, but both Henry VIII and Protector Somerset had needed to retain the league's friendship, since German ports were commonly used for transporting mercenaries to fight in the Scottish and French wars. Freed from foreign wars, Northumberland felt no such constraint and readily acted in defence of England's commercial interests. Mary, too, listened to the Adventurers' complaints against the Hanse and took action on their behalf. Although she had restored the Hanse's privileges on her accession, probably because of the involvement of some Merchant Adventurers in the attempted coup to place Lady Jane Grey on the throne, her government after 1555 revoked them again and placed restraints on the Hanse's involvement in the cloth trade. The Adventurers had shown Mary loyalty during Wyatt's Rebellion, and this was their reward. By the accession of Elizabeth, therefore, the Hanse merchants were finding themselves economically squeezed in England, to the delight of the Adventurers.[3]

Anglo-Burgundian trade soon recovered from the crash of 1551 and 1552, but political events were to disrupt it again under Elizabeth. Right from the start of the reign, relations between Elizabeth and Margaret of Parma, Philip II's regent in the Netherlands, had been tense. The queen's re-establishment of Protestantism had caused considerable disquiet at Brussels, where it was feared that English merchants would protect heretics and smuggle Protestant literature into the Netherlands. English piracy in the Channel during the 1562 French war was another source of grievance. Most important of all, Margaret was dismayed by the recent rise in customs tariffs on English cloth. In May 1558 Mary had introduced a new Book of Rates which had hiked up the duty on cloth by some 500 per cent. Elizabeth's officials were proving so successful in collecting it that the price of English cloth for the Flemish manufacturers had risen correspondingly. Margaret issued a list of complaints about these and other matters but no remedies were suggested by the English government. The regent therefore, decided upon tough tactics to extract concessions from the queen. Recalling how Wolsey had been forced to climb down in 1528, she concluded that an embargo on English cloth would serve to remind England of the value of Habsburg amity and force Elizabeth to meet her demands. With this in mind, she placed a temporary ban on English traders entering her ports in November 1563. She excused her action by claiming it was for the purpose of preventing contagion from the plague then sweeping across England, but no-one was fooled since the epidemic was already past its worst. Nor did the stratagem work. Even before the embargo English merchants, backed by the government, had been looking for an additional mart to decrease dependence on Antwerp, and in January 1564 an agreement was reached with Emden. Antwerp, therefore, suffered more than England from the suspension of trade, and the regent was forced into making peace at virtually any price; she dropped all her immediate demands and on 1 January 1565 traffic was restored unconditionally. To strengthen Anglo-Burgundian amity both sides agreed to refer the disputes between the two sides to a conference which met at Bruges in early 1565 (but which ended inconclusively).[4]

The embargo of 1563–4 reinforced doubts about England's reliance on the Antwerp staple. Several in the government, including Cecil, perceived that 'it were better for this realm for many considerations, that the commodities of the same were issued out rather to sundry places than to one, and specially to such one as the lord thereof is of so great power, as he may therewith annoy this realm by way of a war'.[5] Most English traders, however, were not swayed by this argument and flocked back to Antwerp in 1565 because their sales at Emden had been paltry, owing to the hostility of the Hanse. Elizabeth was equally keen to see the restoration of commerce with Antwerp, for her customs revenues had declined significantly during the period of the embargo. The successful resumption of the Antwerp mart was, however, short-lived. In 1566 the Netherlands were suddenly shaken by political and social disturbances which destroyed business confidence and encouraged the Merchant Adventurers, with government support, to look for a new mart. Admittedly, the summer riots of 1566 had little impact on the English cloth trade as few English merchants were actually present in Antwerp when they took place. On the other hand, the restoration of Spanish authority was accompanied by a flight from the town of native traders, businessmen and artisans fearing prosecution. Further unrest was also feared by members of the English business community. Gresham, for example, warned Cecil in September 1566 that 'this mater is not yet ended but like to come to great mischef'. Indeed, he was so concerned about the future that he advised Cecil that the government should 'do verie well in time to consider some other realme and place' for selling English goods.[6] Shortly afterwards the secretary of the Company went to Hamburg to assess its potential as a mart and in March 1567 a three-man delegation set off for the city to negotiate the establishment of a staple there. After the arrival of the Duke of Alva in Brussels the following summer, this precaution looked particularly sensible. The duke was widely considered to be hostile to the English community of merchants in Antwerp, and rumours abounded that 'there is some great mischief meant towards us'. In particular the Adventurers feared that they would lose their preferential tax rates and be forced to compete on equal terms with other foreign merchants. In fact, the English cloth trade thrived under Alva's firm control. Unfounded though the merchants' suspicions were, they were reported in all seriousness back to the English court and heightened the government's own distrust of Alva.[7]

At one level, the arrest of English merchants and the confiscation of their property in December 1568 as a reprisal for Elizabeth's 'seizure' of the Spanish bullion was totally unexpected; at another, it confirmed the fears of merchants and government alike. Outraged by this hostile act, Elizabeth retaliated in kind. In January 1569 all trade was suspended between England and the countries ruled by the Spanish king. Philip and Alva were horrified by the course of events and hoped to arrange the restoration of trade as quickly as possible. Their initial attempt to reach an agreement with England, however, was mishandled by their hard-line envoy, Christophe d'Assonleville; a second mission by the far more charming and conciliatory Ciappino Vitelli made some progress but his welcome at the English court came to an end with the outbreak of the Northern Rebellion. Indeed, the involvement of the Spanish ambassador in plots against Elizabeth from 1569 to 1571 did much to prevent an early resolution to the crisis. The asylum granted by Alva to her rebels was also deeply resented in England, and Elizabeth was consequently slow to repair the damage to Anglo-Spanish relations. By 1573, however, she was ready to negotiate. Her customs duties from cloth exports had dropped significantly year by year since 1569, while the mart at Hamburg had been struggling to secure a monopoly on English exports. On the political front, her defensive alliance with Charles IX looked less secure after the massacre of the Huguenots in August 1572 and the renewal of civil war in France immediately afterwards. Consequently, Elizabeth allowed Burghley to negotiate for the resumption of trade with Antonio Guaras, a Spanish merchant, who was Alva's intermediary. In March 1573, they reached an agreement based on two principles: that the merchants on both sides should be compensated for their losses; and that neither ruler should give refuge to the other's rebels or protect privateers. This agreement became formalized into the Treaty of Bristol signed in August 1574. The bullion, the source of the original dispute, was returned to the Genoese bankers by 1574.

This time, however, the Merchant Adventurers did not flood back to Antwerp as they had in 1565. Political unrest in the Netherlands now made Antwerp a much less attractive proposition for English merchants. Holland and Zeeland were in full revolt against the Spanish authorities, and the 'Sea Beggars' who in 1572 had established a base in Flushing, at the mouth of the River Scheldt, were attacking all shipping destined for Antwerp. Their piracy did little to endear them to Elizabeth; on the contrary, it encouraged her to view them as dangerous rebels who flouted the law. Even after the Adventurers reached an agreement with the rebel leaders which allowed them to send some shipping freely down the Scheldt, the voyage proved so hazardous that it was abandoned. Instead, merchants landed at Flemish ports and went overland to Antwerp – a more costly and often equally perilous journey. In these conditions, it was not surprising that many of the Adventurers preferred to continue using Hamburg. Anglo-Burgundian trade, therefore, had run into serious difficulties even before the traumatic 'Spanish Fury' (as the three-day sack of Antwerp in November 1576 by mutineering Spanish soldiers came to be known). Nor did it recover after the Spanish troops left the town and a Protestant city council was set up (1577–85). Not only did business seem insecure there, as the whole area was virtually a war zone, but the new authorities imposed high taxes on foreign merchants in order to finance the town's defence. By the time that the English merchants officially left Antwerp in 1582, their commercial activities had trickled to a halt.

There can be little doubt that the rupture of commercial relations between London and Antwerp after 1569 did much to weaken the traditional ties of friendship between England and Spain. No longer did the Adventurers act as a pro-Habsburg lobby on the government; on the contrary, some of them became the loudest anti-Spanish voices within England and keenest backers of privateering exploits against Spain.

(ii) Diversification of Trade within Europe

Second in importance to England's trade with the Netherlands was its commerce in the North and Baltic Seas. Commerce there, however, was severely restricted by the Hanse, who denied English merchants free access to their ports, insisting that their own traders operated as middlemen in all Anglo-Baltic traffic. At the same time, the Hanse defended vigorously their right (granted by Edward IV in 1474) to be exempt from duties on goods they exported from England. This lack of reciprocity infuriated English merchants who contended that they should enjoy the same rights in Hanse cities as Hanse traders enjoyed in England.

The first two Tudors were unsuccessful in their few attempts to enforce the principle of reciprocity. Henry VII tried to break the monopoly of the Hanse outside England by negotiating commercial treaties with Baltic powers (Denmark 1489, Danzig 1491, and Riga 1499), but the commercial advantages from these treaties were limited. In addition, the efforts of both these Tudor kings to erode Hanseatic privileges within England were too spasmodic and ill-sustained to have any lasting impact. Too often the kings' hands were tied by their concern to keep the Hansards' friendship for political reasons. During the 1490s Henry VII had tried to restrict their privileges but in 1504 he restored them all, probably out of fear that otherwise the Hanseatic cities would give support to the de la Pole pretender to the throne. Similarly, in 1522 Henry VIII backed down from a confrontation with the Hanse, against the wishes of the Merchant Adventurers who had petitioned him to impose restraints on Hanseatic trade in England; he too was anxious that otherwise the North German towns would aid an invasion by a de la Pole. Later on in his reign Henry VIII felt unable to challenge the Hanse because of other political considerations: in the 1530s he wanted an alliance with Lübeck and Hamburg against Charles V; and in the 1540s he needed German mercenaries and munitions to be shipped to England from Hanseatic ports.[8]

As already seen, the slump in the demand for English cloth in the Netherlands during 1551 and 1552 spurred on Northumberland to attack the privileges of the Hanse within England. In addition, it led him and Mary to encourage the search for new markets for English cloth. Northumberland's government took some initiatives and had a few successes in the Baltic. Even before the Antwerp crisis, the duke (then Earl of Warwick) had instructed an English agent in the Baltic,

Sir John Borthwick, to negotiate an alliance between the two realms which would be sealed by a marriage of Princess Elizabeth to the son of the Danish king. In May 1552, a commercial treaty with Denmark was under negotiation. Similarly in 1550, discussions 'for a surer amiti touching marchandis' were held with an ambassador of the King of Sweden, and a trade treaty was negotiated in 1551.[9] More significant for the future, however, were his attempts to develop trade further afield, both for the export of English cloth and the import of luxury items by English, rather than foreign, merchants. In 1551 and 1552, ships laden with woollen cloth and other goods visited Morocco, probably for the first time, in voyages financially backed by London merchants and supported by the government. In May 1553, the duke actively encouraged merchants and courtiers to take up shares in a newly formed company established to seek a 'North-East Passage' to China over the northern tip of Scandinavia. Again one of its primary aims was to seek new markets for English cloth, and consequently some 30 per cent of the original investors were cloth exporters. The expedition failed to find a northerly passage to China, but it did open a new commercial route to Muscovy which avoided entering the Baltic and therefore the payment of Sound tolls. The pilot, Richard Chancellor, reached the White Sea and made his way to Moscow where he received a friendly welcome from the tsar, Ivan IV. Up to that point, the Hanse had acted as the middleman for Anglo-Muscovy trade, but Ivan now indicated that he desired to develop direct commercial links with England. On Chancellor's return, Philip and Mary chartered a company to trade in Muscovy and all newly discovered northern lands (1555). In 1557 they negotiated a treaty with Ivan whereby the merchants of both countries would enjoy equal privileges of free trade and protection. To help his English subjects in their search for a North-East Passage (and possibly to divert them from Africa and the Indies) Philip also invited the explorer Stephen Borough to study the charts, notebooks and navigational writings which were deposited in the Spanish archive in Seville.[10]

Both Northumberland and Mary, therefore, had begun to take up the challenge of diversifying into new markets and actively promoted the commercial interests of their merchants working within Europe. Elizabeth built on their work. Like her predecessors, she supported the Merchant Adventurers in their rivalry with the Hanse and restricted the latter's activities in England. Like them too, she tried to find new outlets for English cloth, though in her case the need proved more urgent because of the embargoes of 1563 and 1569. In contrast to them, however, her reign saw a totally new momentum in overseas exploration, as she and her ministers sponsored voyages to all parts of the globe and protected English sea captains when they provoked protests and reprisals from their Iberian rivals.

England's relations with the Hanse reached an all-time low under Elizabeth. Not only did she eventually abolish all the privileges of their traders operating in England, but she also helped her own merchants penetrate the Hanseatic monopoly in the Baltic and North Sea ports. The tone was set at the beginning of the reign. When German envoys arrived in England in April 1560 to petition for the restoration of the Hansards' franchises, they were treated coolly and forced to sign an agreement which did little to improve their position. Because the queen was then at war in Scotland, the Hansards had expected her to offer them concessions in return for an agreement that their ports could be used for the embarkation of mercenaries and the import of munitions. Unlike Henry VIII or Somerset, however, Elizabeth and her Council put the interests of the Merchant Adventurers before short-term political needs, and the Hanseatic envoys left England disappointed.[11] None the less, the Adventurers' animosity towards the Hanse continued unabated, and it was presumably this hostility that led them to turn down Hamburg, a Hanse town, as a site for their staple during the first embargo with the Netherlands. Instead they chose to move to Emden, a town in East Friesland which was not a member of the league. In economic terms, however, the decision was probably a mistake. The Hanse wanted the mart to fail and banned their buyers from attending Emden's fairs, with the result that the Adventurers found difficulty in selling their cloth. Consequently, as soon as trade with the Netherlands was restored, English merchants rushed back to their old haunts. They learned from this mistake. When the political disturbances in the Netherlands forced them to look for new outlets for their cloth, the Adventurers this time chose Hamburg over Emden. In consultation with the government, they signed a ten-year agreement with the city in July 1567 as an insurance measure. Antwerp remained the destination for most of their cloth until the embargo of 1569, at which point the Adventurers quickly transferred their exports to Hamburg. The Hamburg staple was also not ideal. Merchants complained that the Lutheran authorities were intolerant towards their form of religious worship; the town could not take all the English cloth; and the numerous tolls on the River Elbe added to costs. Consequently some merchants, though by no means all, abandoned the city once the embargo was lifted in 1574. Within a year, however, it was clear that the Revolt of the Netherlands was making trade with Antwerp difficult and dangerous. The Adventurers therefore drifted back to Hamburg, but now found a new obstacle to their mart there. The Hanse which had been powerless to prevent the commercial agreement in 1567 had recovered some of its influence in the meantime. In 1577 it successfully applied pressure to Hamburg's council to deny the Adventurers a new agreement, when the old one came up for renewal. The Hanse then intimated to Elizabeth that her subjects could trade freely in its towns only if she restored all the privileges which it had been originally awarded in 1474.[12]

The English government reacted to this commercial blackmail in two ways. First, it encouraged the Adventurers to negotiate for a new mart with Baltic towns outside the Hanse. This had some success. The Company moved its headquarters to Emden in 1579 (to replace the Hamburg mart); it opened a new office in Middleburg in the northern Netherlands in 1582 after Antwerp was finally abandoned; and in 1587 an additional mart was set up in Stade, a commercial rival of Hamburg, also on the Elbe. In addition, Elizabeth encouraged the penetration of English cloth into the Baltic by formally incorporating the Eastland Company in 1579 and allowing any Merchant Adventurer to join on payment of £10. Its base was initially in the Hanseatic town of Danzig but moved to Elbing in East Prussia in 1581.[13] Second, the queen warned the Hanse that its remaining privileges in England would be terminated unless Hamburg agreed to restore those of the Adventurers. When this failed to move them, she kept to her word and stripped the Hanseatic merchants of all their privileges in 1578, leaving them with the status of aliens in England. The Hanse retaliated by working for the expulsion of the Adventurers from Germany, and by co-operating closely with Spain during the war of 1585–1604. The rulers and overlords of Danzig, Emden and Stade were under severe pressure from both the Hanse and Spain to banish the English merchants. The latter left Danzig in 1581 and Emden in 1586, but Stade's economy had so profited from the English staple that its leading citizens ignored all attempts at intimidation. In addition, the Hanse protested to the Emperor Rudolf about the incursions of the Merchant Adventurers into Germany. In 1585 Rudolf unsuccessfully tried to mediate between the two sides; but in 1597 he succumbed to the lobbying from the Hanse, backed up by his Spanish cousins, and expelled the Merchant Adventurers from the Empire as monopolists. In retaliation Elizabeth closed down the Steelyard (the Hanseatic base in London) and expelled Hanseatic merchants from

England.[14] During the war years, the Hanse were also a problem in their role as trade partners and political allies of Spain. Despite their Protestantism, they supplied Philip with the naval stores and victuals he needed to furnish his armadas. All Elizabeth's warnings to them that she considered this commerce to be a hostile act towards her went unheeded. As the Hanse knew, her sailors could neither stop the trade at source nor even intercept it. None the less, her navy could attack Hanse shipping in Iberian harbours and the Portugal Expedition of 1589 resulted in the seizure of some sixty Hanse ships laden with goods. Clearly, the cost of Elizabeth's brave attack on the Hanse had been high and caused the government considerable anxiety during the war years. Only the refusal of the Staders to comply with the imperial ban saved England's vital economic interests in the region.[15]

During the first half of Elizabeth's reign, English trade with Muscovy continued to develop with governmental encouragement and investment, but thereafter it ran into trouble. In 1567 Elizabeth incorporated the Russia Company, and two years later Ivan IV awarded its traders special privileges which effectively gave them exemption from taxes and a monopoly in the interior of Russia. The Company also acquired the sole right to trade overland through Russia with Persia. The tsar hoped for an alliance with Elizabeth against Poland and Sweden as a reward for his concessions, and it took all the queen's diplomatic skills to keep these commercial advantages without yielding to his political demands (backed up by threats). She sent him on average two or three letters a year, sometimes more, and six special embassies between 1566 (the date of the first embassy) and 1584 (the year Ivan died). Despite temporary crises and setbacks, English traders first controlled then dominated the White Sea trade until Ivan's death. Although the trade was not particularly extensive nor profitable, it provided England with vital naval stores. After 1584, however, the Russia Company struggled to maintain its privileges. Its members had long been unpopular in Moscow, but it was only after the end of the Livonian War (1582) that the tsar was strong enough to listen to his own merchants' complaints against them and rescind some of their privileges. The Company's interests were not helped by the attempts of the Habsburgs and their allies to turn the Muscovite rulers against Elizabeth, by accusing her of giving aid to the Turks and King of Poland. In 1589 the Company lost its monopoly over the northern route and for a time there was a danger that its merchants might lose their tax advantages or even be expelled from Russia. Thanks, however, to the patronage of Boris Godunov, Tsar Theodor's most influential minister, who himself became tsar in 1598, the Company retained its presence and remaining privileges in Russia. On the other hand, Godunov was not prepared to give exclusive rights to Englishmen since he saw the benefit from all foreigners trading within his empire. He therefore allowed Dutch and French competitors to trade on equal term with the English, and in the early seventeenth century the latter lost their commercial dominance of the area to the Dutch.[16]

England's special relationship with Ivan IV had been deeply resented by the Hanse and Denmark. The Hanse saw England's expansion into Russia as another example of its commercial aggression at the expense of the North German cities. Furthermore, between 1563 and 1570 they were the allies of Denmark in a war against Russia and accused Elizabeth of supplying their enemy with war materials. This hostility spilled out into the German diet during 1569 when a Protestant league with England came up for discussion. In addition, Denmark had its own particular cause of complaint about England's trade with Russia. By using the northern route English merchants escaped from paying the Sound dues. The Danish king therefore tried to disrupt the English line of communication to the White Sea during the 1560s and 1570s. In the early 1580s, however, Elizabeth wanted an alliance with the king against Spain and the Catholic League in France; and if that were not possible she needed at least Denmark's friendly neutrality. Consequently she was prepared to make some concessions. In 1583 she recognized Danish sovereignty over the northern seas, agreed that the Russia Company would pay a yearly sum to the Danish king for the right to use the northern route, and promised to send no war materials to Russia if war broke out between the two countries.[17]

Though less spectacular than the Muscovy trade, English commerce in the Mediterranean and Levant gained a new impetus under Elizabeth which was to prove far more profitable. In the early Tudor period English traders had operated there but they were absent from the area for twenty years after 1550, a period when Venice dominated the carrying trade. This exclusion from the Mediterranean encouraged English merchants to seek new direct contact with the east to obtain silks, spices and other luxuries; and it was during those years that English merchants first invested in expeditions to Persia and India.[18] Venetian trade, however, was crippled by the War of Cyprus (1570–3) and English shipowners seized the opportunity to fill the vacuum. Their ships re-entered the Mediterranean, trading with Livorno (1573), Sicily (1580) and Marseilles (1590). In 1579 they began to trade directly with Turkey, and a

year later the Sultan granted the English nation a charter of privileges
which put them on an equal commercial footing with the French. From
then onwards English merchants expanded their trade in the Levant, in
particular in Egypt and Syria. As English trading interests grew, a permanent representative in Constantinople became essential, and in 1583
Elizabeth appointed Sir William Harborne to be her ambassador at the
Porte, at her merchants' expense. This move infuriated Philip II, who
feared with some justification that she would use her influence to
encourage the Ottomans to break their truce with Spain. Although the
Turks did not fight in the war as Elizabeth's ally, the profitable trade with
the Levant helped to compensate for the loss of trade elsewhere after
1585, particularly that with the Iberian peninsula.[19]

Anglo-Iberian trade went back to the middle ages and was greatly
stimulated by Henry VII's Treaty of Medino del Campo. It experienced,
however, a setback during the economic recession of the 1550s but was
soon revitalized without any governmental assistance under Elizabeth.
English traders were able to take advantage of a new boom in the Indies
trade by transporting Spanish wool, olive oil, dyes, alum and luxury
items to England, exporting a variety of English products but principally
dyed and finished cloth to Spain and Portugal, and participating in
the lucrative carrying trade between the Iberian peninsula and the Baltic. Like the Antwerp trade, this commerce suffered from the embargoes
of 1563 and 1569, but it fully revived as soon as Spanish ports were
reopened to English ships. As well as its importance to the English economy, this trade had a political significance. The Spanish Company
(formed in 1577) had an obvious vested interest in wanting to promote
harmonious relations with Spain, and acted as a lobby-group on the
English government. During the tense years of the early 1580s the Company did its utmost to prevent an open breach between the two realms.
Thus, it protested strongly to Elizabeth when Francis Drake's circumnavigation of the globe was accompanied by raids on Spanish shipping.
It also warned the queen and Council against supporting Dom António
the pretender to the Portuguese throne. It was only when Philip seques-
tered English shipping in May 1585 that the Company's pleas for peace
became either muted or else converted into cries for reprisals. In the
event, the war destroyed the Spanish Company and many of its members turned instead to privateering. Illicit trade certainly continued, but
the Crown lost valuable customs revenues and by 1598 many in the
Privy Council wanted peace with Spain in order that open commerce
could be resumed.[20]

(iii)   Overseas Exploration, Plunder and Trade[21]

England was a late starter in its interest in Atlantic exploration and trade. Henry VII had been the luke-warm patron of John Cabot and his son Sebastian in their search for new lands to the west, but since their ventures had brought neither financial rewards nor commercial opportunities to their investors, Henry VIII and English merchants had little incentive to supply funds for further speculative voyages. On his return to England, therefore, Sebastian could find no patronage and entered the service of the King of Spain until 1547. It was only with the economic slump of the 1550s that London merchants backed by the Crown saw value in searching for new markets and finding new trade routes overseas.

The first move into extra-European trade, however, was not for the purpose of finding new outlets for English cloth; it was designed to break into the profitable luxury goods trade. In the 1550s some London merchants and shipowners promoted several voyages to Guinea in West Africa, a region within the Portuguese sphere of influence, to bring back gold, ivory and pepper. Initially, this enterprise had the approval of Mary but she was persuaded to ban the trade when Philip upheld the protests of his Portuguese ally. None the less, English trading ships continued to visit Guinea. After 1558, moreover, Elizabeth openly supported these ventures and even invested in some of them. When both the Portuguese and Spanish ambassadors protested to her in 1561 and 1562, she took a firm stand, asserting that she saw no reason why her subjects should not trade in areas where the King of Portugal had dominion, obedience or tribute since 'the use of intercourse of merchandise is chief exercise of amity'. This position Elizabeth consistently upheld throughout the 1560s when her merchants continued to trade in West Africa and also tried to break through the Spanish monopoly in the Indies. Indeed, both Elizabeth and some of her courtiers and ministers (including Leicester) invested in John Hawkins's second slaving voyages of 1564, which bought slaves from West Africa and sold them to Spanish colonists in the Caribbean.[22]

There can be no doubt that Elizabeth's support for her merchants helped create political difficulties with both Spain and Portugal. Both Iberian kings deeply resented the aggressive trading of English seamen and retaliated whenever possible by burning their ships and imprisoning their crews. When Elizabeth's demands for compensation were ignored, there often followed reprisals by both sides. The most notorious incident was that of San Juan de Ulúa in 1568. San Juan was a port on the Gulf of Mexico where Hawkins put in for repairs in September 1568 on his third slaving voyage to the Caribbean. The Spanish authorities attacked him, destroying two of his ships. Rumours of the incident reached England in early December 1568 just after several Spanish vessels carrying bullion on loan from Genoese bankers had taken refuge in English harbours. Historians used to argue that news of the disaster at San Juan encouraged Cecil to order the unloading of the bullion in preparation for its confiscation; and they pointed to the fact that when William Hawkins wrote to Cecil on 3 December about the Spanish attack (and mistakenly his brother's death), he suggested that the pay-ships be seized in reprisal.[23] Most historians now think, however, that the significance of Hawkins's letter has been exaggerated.[24] Even before it had reached Cecil, he had been raising questions about the legal ownership of the treasure. His informers had assured him that the bullion belonged to the Genoese rather than the Spaniards and that Elizabeth could legitimately take over the loan herself and thereby deny the money to Alva in the Netherlands. Clearly, the news of the San Juan incident did not put this idea into Cecil's head. He was at this time preoccupied with the problem of Alva's presence in the Netherlands, rather than the Spanish monopoly in the Indies; but anger at the Spanish attack on Hawkins possibly reinforced his unwillingness to return the treasure and his unhelpfulness when de Spes, the Spanish ambassador, demanded it.[25]

The San Juan affair intensified the anti-Spanish and piratical character of England's overseas exploration and trade. During the rupture with Spain (1569–73) the government allowed this trend to develop. With the queen's approval Francis Drake (a survivor of San Juan) made three voyages to the Panama isthmus in the early 1570s to prey on Spanish shipping and carry out reprisals for San Juan. The peace with Spain, however, led Elizabeth to call off her sea-dogs. In 1574 she revoked a licence which had permitted Sir Richard Grenville to set out towards the southern hemisphere, for fear that it would lead to conflict with Spain. In 1577, however, when relations with Spain had again begun to sour, Elizabeth approved Drake's plan to enter the Pacific through the Magellan straits and explore the west coast of South America south of the area of Iberian occupation. None the less, she kept her support low-key and secret, giving Drake neither a royal commission nor the loan of royal ships. The official purpose of the expedition was to establish colonial settlements in this unoccupied region of the continent, but it was generally expected that Drake would plunder the Spanish Main. The enterprise was financially backed by ministers and courtiers such as Leicester, Walsingham and Hatton, but not Burghley. In fact Drake's voyage failed to establish any colonies but it did turn into a circumnavigation of the globe and was financially very profitable as the Spaniards were robbed of silver bars, gold and coin to the tune of well over £140,000 pounds. On his return to England in September 1580 there were mixed feelings about his achievement. For many he was a hero, but others were highly critical of his piracy, including the London merchants of the Spanish Company and some of the privy councillors, Burghley and the Earl of Sussex. They feared reprisals from Philip II and argued that the treasure should be taken to the Tower and then restored to its owners. Elizabeth disagreed with this approach. In April 1581 she publicly demonstrated her approval of Drake by knighting him on board the *Golden Hind*; she also allowed him to enjoy £10,000, paid back his investors, and used the rest of the money to pay off her debt and invest in the Levant Company. Her provocative action came soon after Spanish troops had holed up in Smerwick and was probably intended to convey a clear signal to Philip that he could not afford to offend her in that way.

Drake's circumnavigation opened up the prospect of direct commercial contact with the East Indies and whetted the English appetite for further plunder of Spanish treasure. At the same time, a further deterioration in Anglo-Spanish relations provided the rationale for new aggressive privateering projects, which had backers within the government. Men like Walsingham and Leicester who favoured a policy of military intervention in the Netherlands recognized that Spain's vulnerability lay in its sea-communications with the Americas. Disruption of these routes by English privateers seemed to them the best way of redressing the military balance within Europe in England's favour. Consequently, in 1581 Walsingham and Leicester favoured schemes proposed by Hawkins and others for an attack on the Azores which had become part of Spain when Philip conquered Portugal. Ultimately, however, Elizabeth vetoed the project as she was not yet convinced that war against Spain was inevitable or desirable. On the other hand she did allow her seamen to accept commissions from Dom António authorizing the plunder of Spanish shipping, and by 1582 at least eleven ships were sailing under his authority. She also agreed to Edward Fenton's voyage to the Moluccas by way of the Cape of Good Hope, but the enterprise (1582–3) foundered when its leaders became sidetracked into plundering the coast of Brazil. None of these privateering ventures were particularly successful. After

Drake's circumnavigation, Philip had tightened up the defences of his South American colonies and effectively barred the English from Panama, Brazil and Peru. The English attacks on shipping also did not hit the Spaniards hard during the early and mid-1580s; on the contrary, Spanish commerce reached a peak in 1585–6.[26]

In the run-up to the outbreak of hostilities with Spain in the Netherlands Elizabeth was bombarded with a variety of ambitious naval projects: for attacking Spanish shipping; establishing English colonies in North America; gaining the Portuguese Spice Islands for Dom António; and attacking the Spanish Newfoundland fishing fleet. At last in 1585 she agreed to a number of maritime ventures to accompany Leicester's land campaign. In the spring of 1585 she ordered Bernard Drake to attack the Spanish fleet in the Newfoundland fisheries. At the same time, she allowed Sir Richard Grenville to set out for Roanoke (Virginia) to establish a colony there, which might be used as a naval base for raids against Spanish shipping. In the summer she licensed Sir Francis Drake to attack Spanish vessels harboured along the Galician coast of northwest Spain and to raid the Spanish treasure fleets in the Caribbean. Again, these activities had only a limited practical effect; Drake captured little booty and established no bases, while the fledgling Roanoke colony was abandoned in June 1586. None the less, the English attacks on Spanish shipping were a cruel blow to Philip II's *reputación* and equally a great morale-booster for the English government. They did as much as Leicester's expedition to persuade Philip to launch his Armada.

The war against Spain influenced the course of England's overseas trade and exploration. Whatever lingering interest remained in establishing commercial contacts with the East, breaking through the Spanish monopoly in the Indies, and planting colonies in the Americas, was lost after 1585 in the privateering war against Spain. Certainly, Walsingham sponsored three voyages of John Davis to the Arctic to search for a 'North-West Passage' between 1585 and 1587, but they were not followed up, even though he had found excellent fishing grounds and claimed to have discovered a route over the Pole. A decade later Sir Walter Raleigh could not obtain the queen's backing for a settlement in Guyana, enticingly designated 'El Dorado'. Instead of investing in overseas expansion, the Crown, merchants, shipowners and gentlemen preferred to put their money into privateering; and every year from 1585 until 1604, between 100 and 200 vessels left England in search of plunder, the annual value of which amounted to between £100,000 and £200,000 and possibly more.[27] At the same time, privateering became the main plank in naval strategy during the war. Dependent as Elizabeth was on private enterprise for her fleets, she had to allow her captains and investors to pursue the type of warfare that would bring them profit. Of course, she herself also benefited from Spanish prizes, and her share was intended to contribute towards the expense of maintaining the 50,000 men serving on the Continent between 1585 and 1597. Thus, in order to satisfy her captains and fill her own war chest Elizabeth sanctioned privateering as an acceptable face of warfare. Although she also intended her naval forces to be used to defend England's shores and destroy potential invasion fleets, once her fleets sailed out to sea they moved beyond her control. As a result practically every naval campaign authorized by the queen for specific strategic ends degenerated into a scramble for spoils. The 1587 attack on Cadiz delayed the sailing of the Armada for a year but Drake could have done so much more had he attacked Santa Cruz's Armada fleet berthed at Lisbon rather than sailed off for the Azores in search of the treasure ships. Similarly, the expedition to Portugal in 1589 sacrificed the wider strategic plan of destroying the remnants of the Armada at Santander and San Sebastian in the interests of finding booty in Lisbon.

During the latter years of the war against Spain, privateering became significantly less profitable. Consequently investors, merchants and sea-captains began to recognize again the value of investing into new commercial ventures overseas. In 1599, for example, some merchants of the Levant Company showed a serious interest in developing trade with the East Indies which had been neglected since the early 1580s. A year later they played a leading part in forming the East India Company which invested in a voyage to the Spice Islands in February 1601. Once peace was signed in 1604 other merchants followed their lead. Not only did further voyages set out for the East, but plans were laid for colonizing Virginia and Barbados. Building on the navigational skills, geographical knowledge and self-confidence acquired during the last quarter of the sixteenth century, Jacobeans took the first faltering steps towards creating a British Empire.

NOTES

1 Introduction

1. This view can be found in J. R. Seeley, *The Growth of British Policy*, vol. i, 2nd edn (Cambridge, 1903); A. F. Pollard, *Henry VIII* (1905); A. F. Pollard, *Wolsey* (1929); R. B. Wernham, *Before the Armada: The Emergence of the English Nation, 1485–1588* (1966).
2. Seeley, *Growth of British Policy*, vol. i, p. 51.
3. James A. Williamson, *The Tudor Age* (1953, 1979), p. 444; J. S. Corbettt, *Drake and the Tudor Navy* (1905), vol. ii, pp. 131, 172.
4. Seeley, *Growth of British Policy*, vol. i, p. 65.
5. E. Lodge, *Illustrations of British History* (1838), vol. ii, p. 87.
6. R. B. Wernham, *The Making of Elizabethan Foreign Policy, 1558–1603* (Berkeley, CA, 1980), p. 72.
7. Hiram Morgan, 'British Policies before the British Isles', in *The British Problem c. 1534–1707: State Formation in the Atlantic Archipelago*, ed. Brendan Bradshaw and John Morrill (1996), p. 68.
8. Steven Gunn, 'The French Wars of Henry VIII', in *The Origins of War in Early-Modern Europe*, ed. J. Black (Edinburgh, 1987), pp. 28–51.
9. David M. Head, 'Henry VIII's Scottish Policy', *The Scottish Historical Review* (hereafter *SHR*), 61 (1982), pp. 1–24.
10. Richard Hoyle, 'War and Public Finance', in *The Reign of Henry VIII: Politics, Policy and Piety*, ed. Diarmaid MacCulloch (Basingstoke, 1995), pp. 84–99; R. S. Schofield, 'Taxation and the Political Limits of the Tudor State', in *Law and Government under the Tudors: Essays Presented to Sir Geoffrey Elton...*, ed. C. Cross, D. Loades and J. J. Scarisbrick (Cambridge, 1988), pp. 227–55.
11. For the Middle Ages, see Nigel Saul, 'England and Europe, Problems and Possibilities', in *England and Europe, 1066–1453*, ed. Nigel Saul (1994) p. 19; Frank Tallett, *War and Society in Early-Modern Europe 1495–1715* (1992), pp. 23, 36–7, 252–3; David Eltis, *The Military Revolution in Sixteenth-Century Europe* (1995), pp. 99–104.
12. Felipe Fernandez-Armesto, *The Spanish Armada: The Experience of War in 1588* (Oxford, 1988), pp. 135–236, 268–71; Simon Adams, *The Armada Campaign of 1588*, New Appreciations in History 13 (1988); Graham Darby, 'The Spanish Armada of... 1597?', *The Historian*, 55 (1997), pp. 14–16.
13. Religion is entirely missing as a theme of foreign policy in P. S. Crowson, *Tudor Foreign Policy* (1973).

14. E. I. Kouri, *England and the Attempts to Form a Protestant Alliance in the Late 1560s: A Case-study in European Diplomacy* (Helsinki, 1981), p. 195.

15. Conyers Read, 'Walsingham and Burghley in Queen Elizabeth's Privy Council', *English Historical Review*, 28 (1913), p. 37. See also Conyers Read, *Mr Secretary Cecil and Queen Elizabeth* (London, 1965) and *Lord Burghley and Queen Elizabeth* (1960).

16. Stephen Alford, 'Reassessing William Cecil in the 1560s', in *The Tudor Monarchy*, ed. John Guy (1997), pp. 237–41; Malcolm R. Thorp, 'William Cecil and the Antichrist: A Study in Anti-Catholic Ideology', in *Politics, Religion, and Diplomacy in Early Modern Europe*, ed. Malcolm R. Thorp and Arthur J. Slavin (Kirksville, MO, 1994), pp. 289–304.

2 Honour and Reputation

1. Machiavelli, *The Prince*, Penguin Classic (1961), p. 119. *The Prince* was written in 1514; English translations appeared in manuscript during Elizabeth I's reign and the first printed translation was published in 1640.

2. Mervyn James, 'English Politics and the Concept of Honour, 1485–1642', *Past and Present*, Suppl. 3 (1978), pp. 3, 10; Malcolm Vale, *War and Chivalry* (1981), pp. 14–5, 22–3; G. Kipling, *The Triumph of Honour* (Leiden, 1977), pp. 11–20, 32–5.

3. S. Gunn, 'The Early Tudor Tournament', in *Henry VIII: A European Court in England*, ed. David Starkey (1991), pp. 47–51; Steven Gunn, 'Chivalry and the Politics of the Early Tudor Court', in *Chivalry in the Renaissance*, ed. Sydney Anglo (Woodbridge, 1990), pp. 107–28.

4. J. J. Scarisbrick, *Henry VIII* (1972), p. 1.

5. Geoffrey Elton, 'War and the English in the Reign of Henry VIII' in *War, Strategy and International Politics: Essays in Honour of Sir Michael Howard*, ed. Lawrence Freedman, Paul Hayes and Robert O'Neill (Oxford, 1992), p. 4.

6. Glenn Richardson, 'Anglo-French Political and Cultural Relations during the Reign of Henry VIII', London University PhD thesis, (1995), p. 25; *Letters and Papers of Henry VIII*, vol. XVIII, i, no. 622; *Letters and Papers of Henry VIII* (hereafter cited as *L & P*) Edward Hall, *Henry VIII*, ed. C. Whibley (1904), pp. 320–7.

7. Roger A. Mason, 'The Scottish Reformation and the Origins of Anglo-British Imperialism', in *Scots and Britons: Scottish Political Thought and the Union of 1603*, ed. Roger A. Mason (Cambridge, 1994), pp. 168–9.

8. *L & P*, vol. I, i, pp. 115, 129; C. S. L. Davies, 'The English People and War in the Early Sixteenth Century', in *Britain and the Netherlands*, vol. VI: *War and Society*, ed. A. C. Duke and C. A. Tamse (The Hague, 1977) p. 1. For the argument that Henry VII's old councillors (Ruthall, Fox and Warham) wanted to keep the peace with France, see Dominic Baker-Smith, '"Inglorious Glory": 1513 and the Humanist Attack on Chivalry', in *Chivalry in the Renaissance*, ed. Sydney Anglo (Woodbridge, 1990), pp. 133–5.

9. *L & P*, vol. I, i, no. 969; *Cal. S. P. Span.*, vol. II, pp. 59–60.

10. Denis Hay (ed.), 'The Anglica Historia of Polydore Virgil AD 1485–1537', *Camden Society*, 3rd series 74 (1950) pp. 175, 181–3; *L & P*, vol. I, i, nos 1286, 1292, 1326, 1327; Hall, pp. 44–51.

11. Hall, pp. 4–6; 'Anglica Historia', pp. 187–8.

12. 'Anglica Historia', p. 197.

13. 'Anglica Historia', p. 163; Helen Miller, *Henry VIII and the Nobility*, pp. 136–7.

14. *L & P*, vol. I, i, nos 1568, 1572, 1588; vol. I, ii, nos 1726, 1728, 1736, 1750, 1822, 1897.

15. *L & P*, vol. I, ii, no. 1844; S. J. Gunn, *Charles Brandon, Duke of Suffolk 1484–1545* (Oxford, 1988), p. 14.

16. Hall, p. 64.

17. *L & P*, vol. II, ii, nos 4137, 4357, 4351; Hall, pp. 165–75. Scarisbrick, *Henry VIII*, pp. 102–6.

18. Joycelyne G. Russell, *Peace-making in the Renaissance*, (1986), pp. 93–6; P. Gwyn, *The King's Cardinal: The Rise and Fall of Thomas Wolsey* (1990), pp. 144–51.

19. *L & P*, vol. III, ii, no. 1508.

20. Hall, p. 229.

21. Gwyn, *Wolsey*, pp. 355, 379.

22. Gunn, 'French Wars', p. 36; Clifford J. Rogers, 'Edward III and the Dialectics of Strategy, 1327–60', *Transactions of the Royal Historical Society* (hereafter *TRHS*), sixth series 4 (1994), pp. 90–1.

23. *L & P*, vol. III, ii, no. 3485; Scarisbrick, *Henry VIII*, p. 177; S. J. Gunn, 'The Duke of Suffolk's March on Paris in 1523', *English Historical Review* (hereafter *EHR*), 101 (1986), pp. 596–634.

24. Gwyn, *Wolsey*, pp. 383–90.

25. William D. Hamilton, 'A Chronicle of England by Charles Wriothesley', *Camden Society*, n. s. 11 (1875), p. 14; G. Bernard, *War Taxation and Rebellion in Early Tudor England: Henry VIII, Wolsey and the Amicable Grant of 1525* (1986), pp. 3, 4; G. W. Bernard and R. W. Hoyle, 'The Instructions for the Levying of the Amicable Grant, March 1525', *Historical Research*, 67 (1994), pp. 190–202. For reactions in Yorkshire and Northumberland to the forced loan of 1522–3, see R. W. Hoyle, 'Letters of the Cliffords: Lords Clifford and the Earls of Cumberland', *Camden Miscellany*, 31, *Camden 4th Series* 44 (1992), pp. 91, 93.

26. *State Papers*, vol. VI, v, p. 480.

27. R. J. Knecht, *Francis I* (Cambridge, 1982), p. 218.

28. For Henry's opportunism, David Potter, 'Foreign Policy', in *The Reign of Henry VIII: Politics, Policy and Piety*, ed. Diarmaid MacCulloch (1995), pp. 119–23. For Henry's financial resources, F. Dietz, *English Public Finance, 1485–1558* (Illinois, 1920), pp. 150–1.

29. *L & P*, vol. XIX, i, nos 700, 730, 741, 786, 816, 817.

30. Hall, pp. 349–50. For details of the French campaign, L. MacMahon, 'The English Invasion of France, 1544', MA thesis, University of Warwick (1992).

31. Samuel Rhea Gammon, *Statesman and Schemer: William, First Lord Paget, Tudor Minister* (Newton Abbot, 1973), pp. 104–7.

32. For Henry II's policy see D. L. Potter, 'Diplomacy in the Mid 16th Century: England and France 1536–1550', PhD thesis, Cambridge University (1973), Chapter 4.

33. The treaty was heavily criticized in W. K. Jordan, *Edward VI: The Threshold of Power* (1968), p. 116. For a more realistic assessment, D. L. Potter (ed.); 'Documents concerning the Negotiations of the Anglo-French Treaty of March 1550', *Camden Miscellany*, 27, *Camden 4th Series* 29 (1984), pp. 58–180. For Paget's views, Gammon, *Paget*, pp. 170–2. 'Wriothesley's Chronicle', vol. I, pp. 35, 39–40.

34. Glenn Richardson, 'Entertainments for the French Ambassadors at the Court of Henry VIII', *Renaissance Studies*, 9 (1995), pp. 404–15.

35. Gwyn, *Wolsey*, pp. 58–82.

36. *Rymer's Foedera*, 13, pp. 624–32; Hall, pp. 170–2, Gwyn, *Wolsey*, p. 98; S. Anglo, *Spectacle, Pageantry and Early-Tudor Policy* (Oxford, 1969), pp. 128–36; G. Mattingly, 'An Early Non-aggression Pact', *Journal of Modern History*, 10 (1938), pp. 1–30; Richardson, 'Entertainments', pp. 405–8.

37. Hall, pp. 174–5.

38. *L & P*, vol. III, i, nos 137, 216; Scarisbrick, *Henry VIII*, pp. 138–9.

39. Hall, *Henry VIII*, pp. 180–218; Anglo, *Spectacle*, pp. 154–69; Richardson, 'Entertainments', pp. 408–10.

40. For the 1522 pageants, see *The Somers Collection of Tracts*, ed. Walter Scott (1809), vol. 1, pp. 32–3.

41. Glenn Richardson, 'Good Friends and Brothers? Francis I and Henry VIII', *History Today*, September 1994, pp. 20–6.

42. A. Francis Steuert (ed.), *Memoirs of Sir James Melville Of Halhill* (London, 1929), pp. 89–99; *Cal. S. P. For. 1562*, p. 15; Anne Somerset, *Elizabeth I* (London, 1992); Antonia Fraser, *Mary Queen of Scots* (London, 1969), pp. 190–2.

43. Scarisbrick, *Henry VIII*, pp. 60–1, 560–7; Head, 'Henry VIII's Scottish Policy', *SHR*, 61 (1982), pp. 1–24.

44. Roger A. Mason, 'Scotching the Brut: Politics, History and National Myth in Sixteenth-Century Britain', in *Scotland and England, 1286–1815*, ed. Roger A. Mason (Edinburgh, 1987), pp. 60–3. It was Patrick Painter, James IV's Secretary, who complained that the English 'despised them'; see Marguerite Wood (ed.), *Flodden Papers*, Scottish Historical Society, 3rd series 20 (1933), p. 322.

45. David Dunlop, 'The Politics of Peace-keeping: Anglo-Scottish Relations from 1503 to 1511', *Renaissance Studies*, 8 (1994) pp. 138–61.

46. Hall, p. 39; R. L. Mackie (ed.), *Letters of James IV, 1505–1513*, Scottish Historical Studies, 3rd series 45 (1953), pp. liii–liv, 273; *L & P*, vol. I, i, no. 974.

47. Hall, p. 95; *James IV Letters*, pp. 268, 293, 302, 320–4; *Flodden Papers*, pp. xliii, 73–9; Norman MacDougall, '"The Greattest Scheip that Ewer Scillit in England or France": James IV's Great Michael', in *Scotland and War A.D. 79–1918*, ed. Norman MacDougall (1991), pp. 47–52. Louis's promised troops were never forthcoming.

48. Hall, pp. 77–82, 95–113. Hall did give a lengthy description of the battle.

49. *James IV Letters*, p. 318.

50. Head, 'Henry VIII's Scottish Policy', pp. 5–18; Hall, p. 321.

51. For Henry's ultimatum, *L & P*, vol. XVII, no. 862. Hall, pp. 320–35; 'Wriothesley's Chronicle', vol. I, pp. 138–42; Margaret Sanderson, *Cardinal of Scotland: David Beaton, c.1494–1546* (Edinburgh, 1986), pp. 63–8; 150–3; Scarisbrick, *Henry VIII*, pp. 552–3, 560–4; Head, 'Scottish Policy', pp. 12–19.

52. *L & P*, vol. XVIII, i, no. 707; ii, no. 481; Head, 'Scottish Policy', pp. 19–24. For Arran, D. Franklin, *The Scottish Regency of the Earl of Arran: A Study in the Failure of Anglo-Scottish Relations* (Lewiston, New York, 1995).

53. *Hamilton Papers*, vol. II, no. 207; 'Wriothesley's Chronicle', vol. I, pp. 147, 16; David H. Caldwell, 'The Battle of Pinkie', in *Scotland and War A.D. 79–1918*, ed. Norman MacDougall (1991), p. 65.

54. For Somerset's policy, M. Bush, *The Government Policy of Protector Somerset* (1975), pp. 7–39; Caldwell, 'The Battle of Pinkie', pp. 66–70.

55. *Cal. S.P. For. 1553–58*, pp. 35, 40; *Cal. S. P. Span. 1554–58*, pp. 288, 293–94; *Cal. S. P. Ven. 1557*, pp. 1067, 1074; C. S. L. Davies, 'England and the French War, 1557–9', in *The Mid-Tudor Polity c.1540–1560*, ed. J. Loach and R. Tittler (1980), pp. 159–61; Harris E. Harbison, *Rival Ambassadors at the Court of Queen Mary* (1940), pp. 309–10, 324; Gammon, *Paget*, pp. 238–40; David Loades, *The Reign of Mary I*, pp. 189–91, 304–8.

56. *Cal. S. P. For. 1562*, pp. 306–7; P. Forbes, *Public Transactions*, vol. II, pp. 48.

57. Forbes, *Public Transactions*, vol. II, pp. 61, 78; J. Malham, *Harleian Miscellany* (London, 1808), pp. 374–9.

58. *Cabala Scrinia Ceciliana* (1663), pp. 109–10; Sir Dudley Digges, *The Compleat Ambassador* (1655), pp. 104, 126–8.

59. Parks and Oldys, *Harleian Miscellany*, vol. I, p. 436.

60. Davies, 'The English People', pp. 10, 14; Ferguson, *Chivalric Tradition*, p. 56; Ben Lowe, 'Peace Discourse and Mid-Tudor Foreign Policy', in *Political Thought and the Tudor Commonwealth: Deep Structure, Discourse and Disguise*, ed. Paul A. Fideler and T. F. Mayer (London, 1992), pp. 109, 112–17; Baker-Smith, 'Humanist Attack on Chivalry', pp. 131, 144; Robert P. Adams, 'Bold Bawdry and Open Manslaughter: The English New Humanist Attack on Medieval Romance', *The Huntington Library Quarterly*, 23 (1959–60), pp. 33–6, 40–1; J. R. Hale, 'Incitement to Violence? English Divines on the Theme of War 1578 to 1631', in *Florilegum Historiale: Essays Presented to Wallace K. Ferguson*, ed. J. G. Rowe and W. H. Stockdale (Toronto, 1971), pp. 372–4. This view would seem to fit in with the more general interpretation of M. E. James that the sixteenth century saw a fundamental shift in culture from an honour-based society to a civil society which valued obedience to the state. James, 'Concept of Honour'.

61. Vale, *Chivalry*, pp. 15–6; Anthony Esler, *The Aspiring Mind of the Elizabethan Younger Generation* (Durham, NC, 1966), p. 79.

62. Esler, *Aspiring Mind*, pp. 87–124; Ferguson, *Chivalric Tradition*, pp. 68–73.

63. Lowe, 'Peace Discourse', pp. 122–4; 'Wriothesley's Chronicle', p. 151; Harbison, *Rival Ambassadors*, pp. 320–8.

3 Security and Defence

1. Examples of border raids and jurisdictional disputes appear in all the Calendars of State Papers. For the general problem of the borders, Steven G. Ellis, *Tudor Frontiers and Noble Power: The Making of the British State* (Oxford, 1995), pp. 25–41.

2. For difficulties over the Debateable Lands, W. Mackay Mackenzie, 'The Debateable Land', *SHR*, 30 (1951), pp. 109–25. For problems of the Scottish border, Thomas I. Rae, *The Administration of the Scottish Frontier, 1513–1603* (Edinburgh, 1966). For the dispute over the monastery, *Acts of the Privy Council*, vol. v, pp. 285, 296; *Cal. S. P. For. Mary, 1553–58*, p. 274, and Harbison, *Rival Ambassadors*, p. 304.

3. R. W. Hoyle, 'Letters of the Cliffords. Lords Clifford and the Earls of Cumberland', *Camden Miscelleny*, 31, 4th Series 44 (1992), pp. 23–9, 44, 47–50.

4. For the French in Ireland, Ciaran Brady, *The Chief Governors: The Rise and Fall of Reform Government in Tudor Ireland, 1536–88* (Cambridge, 1994), pp. 57–9, and David Potter, 'French Intrigue in Ireland During the Reign of Henri II, 1547–1559', *The International History Review*, 5 (1983), pp. 159–80. For general foreign intervention in Ireland, William Palmer, *The Problem of Ireland in Tudor Foreign Policy, 1485–1603* (Woodbridge, 1994).

5. David Dunlop, 'The Politics of Peace-keeping: Anglo-Scottish Relations from 1503 to 1511', *Renaissance Studies*, 8 (1994), pp. 138–61; Norman Mac-Dougall, *James IV* (Edinburgh, 1989), pp. 22–8; *Flodden Papers*, pp. xviii, xxiv; *L &P*, vol. i, i, nos 114, 129, 153, 684. For James's ultimatum, Hall, pp. 77–80.

6. Marcus Merriman, 'The High Road from Scotland: Stewarts and the Tudors in the Mid-Sixteenth Century', in *Uniting the Kingdom? The Making of British History*, ed. Alexander Grant and Keith J. Stringer (1995), pp. 114–5.

7. Head, 'Henry VIII's Scottish Policy', pp. 3–8; Richard Glen Eaves, *Henry VIII and James V's Regency, 1524–1528: A Study in Anglo-Scottish Diplomacy* (1987), p. 19.

8. Head, 'Henry VIII's Scottish Policy', pp. 8–14; 'Clifford Letters', p. 163.

9. For logistical difficulties, Merriman, 'The High Road from Scotland', in *Uniting the Kingdom?* pp. 116–17.

10. M.L. Bush, *The Government Policy of Protector Somerset* (1975), pp. 7–39; Caldwell, 'Battle of Pinkie', pp. 61–89; Elizabeth Bonner, 'The Recovery of St Andrews Castle in 1547: French Naval Policy and Diplomacy in the British Isles', *EHR*, 111 (1996), pp. 578–98; Jenny Wormold, *Mary Queen of Scots: A Study in Failure* (1991), pp. 60–3; M. H. Merriman, 'Mary Queen of France' in *Mary Stewart, Queen in Three Kingdoms*, ed. Michael Lynch (Oxford, 1988), pp. 38–41.

11. Potter, 'French Intrigue', pp. 161–75.

12. Wormold, *Mary Queen of Scots*, pp. 81–6.

13. *A. P. C.*, vol. v, p. 94; *Cal. S. P. For. Mary*, pp. 43, 47, 158,166, 232, 267, 275, 276, 279–80.

14. *Cal. S. P. Dom. Add. 1547–65*, pp. 449, 453, 456–7, 463, 473.

15. Loades, *Reign of Mary*, pp. 310–11.

16. *Cal. S. P. For. Mary*, pp. 310–11, 316, 321, 325, 350, 351–3. For Grey's letter of 27 December, *An English Garner: Tudor Tracts, 1532–1588*, ed. A. F. Pollard (New York, 1964), pp. 303–5.

17. Contemporary accounts of the fall of Calais and Guisnes appear in *An English Garner*, pp. 290–301, 306–32. See also, Davies, 'The French War', pp. 168–78, and David Potter, 'The Duc de Guise and the Fall of Calais, 1557–58', *EHR*, 98 (1983), p. 483.

18. M. J. Rodriguez-Salgado, *The Changing Face of Empire: Charles V, Philip II and Habsburg Authority, 1551–1559* (Cambridge, 1988), pp. 310–18.

19. Jane A. Dawson, 'William Cecil and the British Dimension of Early Elizabethan Foreign Policy', *History*, 74 (1989), pp. 200–1.

20. Anne I. Cameron (ed.), *The Scottish Correspondence of Mary of Lorraine*, Scottish History Society, 3rd Series 10 (Edinburgh, 1927), pp. 419, 428–9; HMC 9 *Salisbury*, vol. i, pp. 165–7.

21. J. Payne-Collier (ed.), 'The Egerton Papers', *Camden Society*, 12 (1840), pp. 30–4.

22. Morgan 'British Policies before the British State', in *The British Problem c. 1534–1707*, p. 78.

23. S. Haynes, *Cecil State Papers* (1740), pp. 217, 224, 230, 235.

24. HMC 9 *Salisbury*, vol. i, pp. 191, 207; PRO SP12/7 f.185. Only the Earl of Arundel registered his dissent, though five other councillors expressed some doubt.

25. HMC 9 *Salisbury*, vol. i, pp. 181, 187–9.

26. Dawson, 'William Cecil and the British Dimension', pp. 196–216; Jane E. A. Dawson, 'Two Kingdoms or Three? Ireland in Anglo-Scottish Relations in the Middle of the Sixteenth Century', in *Scotland and England*, ed. Roger A. Mason (1987) pp. 113–31.

27. Mason, '"Scotching the Brut"', pp. 71–2; A. H. Williamson, *Scottish National Consciousness in the Age of James VI* (Edinburgh, 1979), pp. 11–16.

28. Jane E. A. Dawson, 'Mary Queen of Scots, Lord Darnley, and Anglo-Scottish Relations in 1565', *The International History Review*, 8 (1986), pp. 4–24; Simon Adams, 'The Release of Lord Darnley and the Failure of the Amity', in *Mary Stewart, Queen in Three Kingdoms*, ed. Michael Lynch (Oxford, 1988), pp. 123–53.

29. *Cabala Scrinia Ceciliana* (1603), pp. 115–18, 125.

30. For the policies of the two Scottish factions, E. Lodge, *Illustrations of British History*, vol. i, (1838), pp. 458–61. For the 1568 proceedings against Mary, G. Donaldson, *The First Trial of Mary Queen of Scots* (1969).

31. PRO SP 59/16 f. 169; SP 52/17 f. 130.

32. BL Cotton, MS Caligula, Cii, ff. 201–2.

33. PRO SP 52/18, ff. 72, 73; BL Cotton, MS Caligula, Cii, ff. 214.

34. BL Cotton, MS Caligula, Cii, ff. 334, 338; PRO SP 59/17 f. 95; *Cal. Scot. P. 1569–71*, pp. 344–6.

35. *Cal. S. P. Scot. 1571–74*, p. 1; Read, *Lord Burghley*, pp. 23, 103.

36. *Cal. S. P. For 1575–77*, p. 31.

37. M. Leiman, 'Sir Francis Walsingham and the Anjou Marriage Plan 1574–81', PhD thesis, Cambridge University (1989), p. 58.

38. For Elizabeth's negotiations with James, John Bruce (ed.), 'Letters of Queen Elizabeth and King James VI of Scotland', *Camden Society*, 46 (1849). For Elizabeth's policy towards Scotland after 1572, see Keith M. Brown, 'The Price of Friendship: The "Well Affected" and English Economic Clientage in Scotland before 1603', in *Scotland and England*, ed. Roger A. Mason (1987), pp. 139–63; Wallace T. MacCaffrey, *Queen Elizabeth and the Making of Policy, 1572–1588* (Princeton, NJ, 1981), pp. 402–27.

39. *Cal. S.P. For. 1571–72*, pp. 422–3.

40. Palmer, *The Problem of Ireland*, pp. 111–15.

41. Cited in Palmer, *The Problem in Ireland*, p. 135.

42. Hiram Morgan, *Tyrone's Rebellion: The Outbreak of the Nine Years War in Tudor Ireland* (Woodbridge, 1993), pp. 114–15, 206–13.

43. John J. Silke, *Kinsale* (Liverpool, 1970), pp. 82–146; Morgan, 'British Policies before the British Isles', in *The British Problem c.1534–1707*, p. 85.

44. Morgan, 'British Policies', p. 69; Levine, *Tudor Dynastic Problems*, pp. 177–8.

45. *Letters of James IV*, p. xxxviii.

46. *L & P*, vol. ii, ii, nos 809, 2113; iii, i, nos 1221, 2340, 2708, 2768, 2870, 3224, 3447.

47. G. W. Bernard, 'The Tudor Nobility in Perspective', p. 13; Susan Brigden, 'Sir Thomas Wyatt and Sir Francis Bryan', *Historical Journal*, (1996), pp. 8–9; Christoph Hollger, 'Reginald Pole and the Legations of 1537 and 1539: Diplomatic and Polemical Responses to the Break with Rome', DPhil, University of Oxford (1989); T. F. Mayer, 'A Diet for Henry VIII: The Failure of Reginald Pole's 1537 Legation', *Journal of British Studies*, 26 (1987), pp. 305–31.

48. Wernham, *Before the Armada*, pp. 98–101; Crowson, *Tudor Foreign Policy*, pp. 6, 90–101.

49. Indeed Mary's betrothal to the *dauphin* was broken as a result of the Imperial alliance.

50. 'The History of Wyatt's Rebellion' by John Proctor, printed in *Tudor Tracts*, pp. 209, 212–3.

51. For Elizabeth's matrimonial negotiations, Susan Doran, *Monarchy and Matrimony: The Courtships of Elizabeth I* (1996).

52. *Cal. S. P. Ven. 1557*, p. 1067.

53. *Cal. S. P. For. 1558–59*, pp. 131, 156–7, 559.

54. Levine, *Tudor Dynastic Problems*, p. 178; Adams, 'The Release of Lord Darnley', pp. 123–53. For a different perspective, Dawson, 'Anglo-Scottish Relations in 1565', pp. 4–24.

55. Dawson, 'Anglo-Scottish Relations in 1565', pp. 4–24; MacCaffrey, *Elizabethan Regime*, pp. 114–22, 130–4; Read, *Mr Secretary Cecil*, pp. 338–46.

56. *Cal. S. P. For. 1562*, p. 55; Forbes, *Public Transactions*, vol. ii, pp. 2, 24, 61, 149.

57. John H. Pollen (ed.), *Papal Negotiations with Mary Queen of Scots during her Reign in Scotland 1561–67*, Scottish History Society (Edinburgh, 1901), pp. 173–90; Doran, *Monarchy and Matrimony*, pp. 76–98.

58. Although many historians have stated that Philip was lukewarm about the plot, Professor Parker draws upon evidence in the AGS Estado manuscripts at Simancas to argue otherwise. See C. Martin and G. Parker, *The Spanish Armada* (1988), pp. 88, 281.

59. M. J. Rodriguez-Salgado, 'The Anglo-Spanish War: The Final Episode in the "Wars of the Roses"?'in *England, Spain and the Gran Armada, 1585–1604*, ed. M. J. Rodriguez-Salgado and Simon Adams (Edinburgh, 1991), pp. 9–20.

60. P. J. Holmes, 'Mary Stewart in England', in *Mary Stewart, Queen in Three Kingdoms*, ed. Michael Lynch (Oxford, 1988), pp. 195–215.

61. Julian Lock, 'Strange Usurped Potentates: Elizabeth I, the Papacy and the Indian Summer of the Medieval Deposing Power', DPhil, University of Oxford (1992), pp. 141–4.

62. Malcolm Thorp, 'Catholic Conspiracy in Early Elizabethan Foreign Policy', *Sixteenth Century Journal*, 15 (1984), pp. 431–44; Lock, 'Strange Usurped Potentates', DPhil, Oxford, pp. 78–81.

63. For Elizabeth's reaction, *Cal. S. P. Span. 1558–67*, pp. 583, 589–90, 610, 659, 671.

64. Julio Retamal Favereau, 'Anglo-Spanish Relations, 1566–72: The Mission of Don Guerau de Spes at London, with a Preliminary Consideration of that of Mr John Man at Madrid', DPhil, University of Oxford (1972), pp. 98–113.

65. These events can be followed in G. Parker, *The Dutch Revolt, 1548–1648* (1977) and MacCaffrey, *Making of Policy, 1572–88*, pp. 217–66.

66. HMC 9 *Salisbury*, vol. II, p. 244.

67. For the Anjou marriage negotiations and its significance in foreign policy, Doran, *Monarchy and Matrimony*, pp. 146–94.

68. *Cal. S. P. For. 1584–85*, pp. 149–50, 250, 315–6.

69. *Cal. S. P. For. 1584–55*, pp. 149–50, 465, 521, 571; Simon Adams, 'The Outbreak of the Elizabethan Naval War against the Spanish Empire: The Embargo of May 1585 and Sir Francis Drake's West Indies Voyage', in *England, Spain and the Gran Armada, 1585–1604* (Edinburgh, 1991), pp. 45–63.

70. Fernandez-Armesto, *The Spanish Armada*, pp. 41–5; Lock, 'Strange Usurped Potentates', DPhil, Oxford, p. 451; T. Wright, *Queen Elizabeth and Her Times* (1838), vol. ii, p. 391.

71. *Cal. S. P. For. 1584–85*, pp. 416, 433, 447–8, 557, 566–7, 636–9; Read, *Lord Burghley*, pp. 382–6.

72. For the policy and campaigns in France, S. Adams, 'The Protestant Cause: Religious Alliance with the European Calvinist Communities as a Political Issue in England 1585–1630', DPhil, University of Oxford (1973), pp. 104–47; Wallace T. MacCaffrey, *Elizabeth I: War and Politics 1588–1603* (New Jersey, 1992) pp. 137–95; *List and Analysis of State Papers, Foreign Series: Elizabeth I*, ed. Richard Bruce Wernham, *1590–91*, pp. 262, 529; *1593–94*, pp. 196, 387, 410; *1595* pp. 96–7, 158–9.

73. For criticisms, C. Wilson, *Queen Elizabeth and the Revolt of the Netherlands* (1970); G. Ramsey, 'The Foreign Policy of Elizabeth I', in *The Reign of Elizabeth I*, ed. Christopher Haigh (1984), pp. 147–68.

4 Religion

1. A. F. Pollard, *Wolsey* (1929), pp. 121–2, 161–4, 330–2; D. S. Chambers, 'Cardinal Wolsey and the Papal Tiara', *Bulletin of the Institute of Historical Research*, 38 (1965), pp. 20–30; Scarisbrick, *Henry VIII*, p. 73.

2. Scarisbrick, *Henry VIII*, pp. 55–6; 'Anglica Historia', pp. 161, 163; *L & P*, vol. I, i, no. 974; *James IV Letters*, p. 307.

3. W. E. Wilkie, *The Cardinal Protectors of England: Rome and the Tudors before the Reformation* (Cambridge, 1974), pp. 110–13.

4. Scarisbrick, *Henry VIII*, pp. 158–60; Gwyn, *Wolsey*, pp. 156–7.
5. R. J. Knecht, *Francis I* (Cambridge, 1982), pp. 206–20; Scarisbrick, *Henry VIII*, pp. 263–306.
6. Scarisbrick, *Henry VIII*, pp. 241–63.
7. Lock, 'Strange Usurped Potentates', DPhil, Oxford, pp. 125–56.
8. Heinrich Lutz, 'Cardinal Reginald Pole and the Path to Anglo-Papal Mediation at the Peace Conference of Marq, 1553–55' in *Politics and Society in Reformation Europe*, ed. E. I. Kouri and Tom Scott (1987), pp. 329–49.
9. *Cal. S. P. Ven. 1556–57*, nos 772, 792.
10. Loades, *The Reign of Mary Tudor*, pp. 230–3, 349–50, 428–36.
11. C. G. Bayne, *Anglo-Roman Relations, 1558–1565* (Oxford, 1913), pp. 1–61.
12. Doran, *Monarchy and Matrimony*, pp. 47–51; for the Privy Council's answer to representation at Trent, PRO SP 70/26, f. 21.
13. Bayne, *Anglo-Roman Relations*, pp. 117–21, 206–17.
14. Lock, 'Strange Usurped Potentates', pp. 404–6; Wright, *Elizabeth I and her Times*, vol. i, p. 379.The nuncio used the excuse of a cold but made his feelings plain. *Cal. S. P. Rome 1572–78*, pp. 70, 79, 87.
15. Lock, 'Strange Usurped Potentates', p. 451.
16. L. von Pastor, *The History of the Popes*, xxi, p. 270; Fernandez-Armesto, *The Spanish Armada*, p. 47.
17. Patrick MacGrath, *Papists and Puritans under Elizabeth I* (1967), pp. 293, 296.
18. Rory McEntegart, 'England and the League of Schmalkaden 1531–47: Faction, Foreign Policy and the English Reformation', PhD, University of London, 1992, pp. 36–75; Neelak Serawlook Tjernagel, *Henry VIII and the Lutherans: A Study in Anglo-Lutheran Relations from 1521 to 1547* (St Louis, Mo, 1965), pp. 128–34; Jörg Engelbrecht, 'Anglo-German Relations in the Reign of Henry VIII', in *Henry VIII in History, Historiography and Literature*, ed. Uwe Baumann (Frankfurt, 1992), pp. 117–18; T. H. Lloyd, *England and the German Hanse, 1157–1611: A Study of their Trade and Commercial Diplomacy* (Cambridge, 1991), pp. 260–3.
19. McEntergart, 'England and the League of Schmalkalden', pp. 219–85.
20. *L & P*, vol. xiv, i, nos 490, 580, 1260.
21. Engelbrecht, 'Anglo-German Relations', pp. 121–4; Rory McEntergart, 'Henry VIII and the Marriage to Anne of Cleves', in *Henry VIII: A European Court in England*, ed. David Starkey (1991), pp. 140–4.
22. McEntergart, 'England and the League of Schmalkalden', pp. 466–71.
23. *A.P.C.*, vol. ii, pp. 60–1; Diarmaid MacCulloch, *Thomas Cranmer* (Yale, 1996), pp. 380–1.
24. *Cal. S. P. Span. 1547–49*, pp. 218, 394–5, 410–20.
25. J. G. Nichols, *Literary Remains of King Edward VI* (1857), vol. ii, pp. 357, 366–7, 405–7.
26. PRO SP 12/12, f. 6; SP 70/20, f. 110; BL Addit., MS 35831, f. 22; Wright, *Queen Elizabeth*, vol. i, pp. 96–7; *Cal. S. P. For. 1561–62*, p. 562; *1562*, pp. 276, 280–1, 301, 467.
27. *Cal. S. P. For. 1562*, pp. 488, 514. Details of the negotiations with the Germans in the late 1560s are to be found in Kouri, *Attempts to Form a Protestant Alliance*.
28. *Cal. S. P. For. 1572–74*, p. 449; *1575–77*, p. 610; *1578–79*, p. 38.

29. *Cal. S.P. For. 1584–85*, pp. 135, 151, 208–9, 416, 433, 447–8, 557, 556–7, 636–9; *1585–86*, pp. 255–7.

30. MacCulloch, *Cranmer*, pp. 113–4, 161.

31. Bush, *Government Policy of Protector Somerset*, pp. 21–2; Merriman, 'The High Road from Scotland', in *Uniting the Kingdom?*, p. 122.

32. Wormald, *Mary Queen of Scots*, pp. 73–5; Mason, 'The Scottish Reformation', in *Scots and Britons*, pp. 170–5.

33. Marcus Merriman, 'War and Propaganda during the Rough Wooing', *Scottish Tradition*, 9–10 (1979–80), pp. 20–30; 'The Assured Scots', *SHR*, 47 (1968), pp. 13–14, 21–34; Dawson, 'Cecil and Foreign Policy', pp. 196, 198. See also Jane Dawson, 'Anglo-Scottish Protestant Culture and Integration in Sixteenth-Century Britain', in *Conquest and Union: Fashioning a British State 1485–1725*, ed. Steven G. Ellis and Sarah Barber (Harlow, 1995), pp. 87–114. My scepticism towards Dawson's argument can be seen in Chapter 3, pp. 51–2.

34. Adams, 'The Protestant Cause', DPhil, Oxford, pp. 24, 111; 'A Treatise of England's Perils, 1578', *Archiv für Reformations Geschichte*, 46 (1955), pp. 246–9.

35. Paul E. J. Hammer, 'Patronage at Court, Faction and the Earl of Essex', in *The Reign of Elizabeth I: Court and Culture in the Last Decade*, ed. John Guy (1995), pp. 79, 80–1, 85–6; Adams, 'The Protestant Cause', pp. 110–11.

36. Thorp, 'William Cecil and the Antichrist', p. 290; Read, *Lord Burghley*, p. 91; Hatfield MS 148, f. 23; PRO SP12/51, ff. 6–7.

37. P. Collinson 'England, 1558–1640', in *International Calvinism, 1541–1715*, ed. Menna Prestwich (Oxford, 1986), p. 203.

38. For France, *Cal. S. P. For. 1562*, pp. 24, 164; *Harleian Miscellany*, vol. I, p. 377, BL Cotton MS Fvi, f. 248, PRO SP 70/127, ff. 228–30; *Lists and Analysis of S. P. For. 1593–4*, pp. 372–3, 378. For the Netherlands, *Cal. S. P. Span. 1568–79*, pp. 598, 601.

39. *Cal. S. P. Span. 1558–67*, pp. 552–3; *1568–79*, p. 7; *Cabala*, p. 721.

40. For disagreements with the States-General, Tracey Borman, 'Untying the Knot? The Survival of the Anglo-Dutch Alliance 1587–97', *European History Quarterly*, 27 (1997), pp. 307–37.

5 Commerce

1. The Company was based in London but had separate companies in the greater ports. See Douglas R. Bisson, *The Merchant Adventurers of England: The Company and the Crown, 1474–1564* (Newark, NJ, 1993), pp. 1–31; Wolf-Rüdiger Baumann, *The Merchant Adventurers and the Continental Cloth Trade* (Berlin, 1990), pp. 1–3.

2. S. J. Gunn, 'Wolsey's Foreign Policy and the Domestic Crisis of 1527–8', in *Cardinal Wolsey, Church, State and Art*, ed. S. J. Gunn and P. Lindley (Cambridge, 1991), pp. 149–77.

3. T. H. Lloyd, *England and the German Hanse, 1157–1611: A Study of their Trade and Commercial Diplomacy* (Cambridge, 1991), pp. 66–98; *Cal. S. P. For. Mary*, p. 216.

4. G. D. Ramsey, *The Queen's Merchants and the Revolt of the Netherlands: The End of the Antwerp Mart* (Manchester, 1986), pp. 10–15.
5. Conyers Read, *Mr Secretary Cecil*, pp. 295–6.
6. Lettenhove, *Relations Politiques*, vol. IV, pp. 352–4.
7. For this and later paragraphs, see Ramsey, *Queen's Merchants*.
8. Bisson, *Merchant Adventurers*, pp. 48–55; Lloyd, *England and the German Hanse*, pp. 251–9; Tjernagel, *Henry VIII and the Lutherans*, pp. 128–34.
9. Instructions to Borthwick, BL Sloane MS 2442 f. 27; *Literary Remains of Edward VI*, vol. II, pp. 255, 260; *Cal. S. P. Span. 1549–52*, pp. 63, 526; *1554–58*, pp. 379–80.
10. Kenneth R. Andrew, *Trade, Plunder and Settlement: Maritime Enterprise and the Genesis of the British Empire 1480–1630* (Cambridge, 1984), pp. 65, 101–2, Loades, *Tudor Navy*, pp. 156, 76; Henryk Zins, *England and the Baltic in the Elizabethan Era* (Manchester, 1972), pp. 35–8; *Cal. S. P. For. Mary*, p. 300.
11. G. D. Ramsey, *The City of London in International Politics at the Accession of Elizabeth Tudor* (Manchester, 1975), pp. 158–60.
12. Lloyd, *England and the German Hanse*, pp. 314–28.
13. Elbing had effectively broken away from the Hanse. Zins, *England and the Baltic*, p. 58. For Stade and the hostility of the Hanse, see G. D. Ramsey, 'The Settlement of the Merchant Adventurers at Stade, 1587–1611' in *Politics and Society in Reformation Europe*, ed. E. I. Kouri and Tom Scott (1989), pp. 452–67.
14. Lloyd, *England and the German Hanse*, pp. 323–40; Baumann, *Merchant Adventurers*, pp. 15–16.
15. Zins, *England and the Baltic*, p. 56; Ramsey, 'The Merchant Adventurers at Stade', pp. 459–67.
16. Inna Lubimenko, 'The Correspondence of Queen Elizabeth with the Russian Czars', *American Historical Review*, 19 (1914), pp. 525–4; 'Egerton Papers', *Camden Society*, 12 (1840), pp. 288–92; T. S. Willan, *The Early History of the Russia Company, 1553–1603* (Manchester, 1956), pp. 174, 179, 225.
17. Zins, *England and the Baltic*, pp. 43–7, 63–4; Willan, *Russia Company*, pp. 157–9.
18. Robert Brenner, *Merchants and Revolution: Commercial Change, Political Conflict and London Overseas Traders, 1550–1653* (Cambridge, 1993), pp. 13–14.
19. Andrews, *Trade, Plunder and Settlement*, pp. 88–93, 97.
20. Pauline Croft, 'English Commerce with Spain and the Armada War, 1558–1603', in *England, Spain and the Gran Armada, 1585–1604*, pp. 237–63.
21. I would like to thank Dr John C Appleby for allowing me to read his chapter 'War, Politics and Colonization, 1558–1625' before publication.
22. *Cal. S. P. For. Mary*, p. 198; *Cal. S. P. For. 1562*, p. 54; J. W. Blake, *West Africa: Quest for God and Gold 1454–1578* (1977), pp. 155–6, 163–4, 173–5; Andrews, Trade, *Plunder and Settlement*, p. 122.
23. R. Pollitt, 'John Hawkins's Troublesome Voyages: Merchants, Bureaucrats and the Origins of the Slave Trade', *Journal of British Studies*, 12 (1973), pp. 26–40.
24. Some (unconvincingly in my view) go further and deny that Cecil had any plans to keep the treasure. See Ramsey, 'Foreign Policy of Elizabeth I', in *The Reign of Elizabeth I*, p. 93.

25. Favereau, 'Anglo-Spanish Relations 1566–72', DPhil Oxon, pp. 101–4.
26. D. B. Quinn and A. N. Ryan, *England's Sea Empire, 1550–1642* (1983), pp. 138–9; Adams, 'The Outbreak of the Elizabethan Naval War', in *England, Spain and the Gran Armada*, pp. 50–3.
27. Andrews, *Trade, Plunder and Settlement*, pp. 179–82, 359; K. R. Andrews, *Elizabethan Privateering: English Privateering during the Spanish War, 1585–1603* (Cambridge, 1964), pp. 32–4, 128–34.

BIBLIOGRAPHY

This bibliography is intended as a guide for further reading. It only lists the works cited most frequently in the text, together with books providing good general accounts of foreign policy. All books are printed in London unless otherwise stated.

Printed Sources

All works on English foreign policy depend heavily on the State Papers in the Public Record Office. The *printed Calendars* are invaluable.

Calendar of State Papers, Foreign, Edward, Mary and Elizabeth, ed. W. Turnbull and J. Stevenson (1861–3).
Calendar of State Papers Relating to Scotland and Mary, Queen of Scots, 1547–1603, ed. J. Bain (1898–1969).
Calendar of State Papers Spanish, ed. G. A. Bergenroth, P. de Gayángos and M. A. S. Hume (1862–99).
Calendar of State Papers Venetian, ed. R. Brown and G. C. Bentinck (1864–90).

Useful *chronicles* include:

Hall, Edward, *Henry VIII*, ed. C. Whibley (1904).
Hay, Denis (ed.), 'The Anglica Historia of Polydore Virgil AD 1485–1537', *Camden Society*, 3rd series, 74.
Hamilton, William D. (ed.), 'A Chronicle of England by Charles Wriothesley', vol. i, *Camden Society*, n. s. 11 (1875).
Nichols, J. G., *Literary Remains of King Edward VI* (1857).

Amongst the many invaluable *collections of documents* which contain letters and other relevant materials, the following have been widely consulted:

Brewer, J. S., *et al.*, *Letters and Papers, Foreign and Domestic, of the Reign of Henry VIII*, 21 vols (1862–1910), Addenda (1929–32).

Bruce, John (ed.), 'Letters of Queen Elizabeth and King James VI of Scotland', *Camden Society*, 46 (1849).

Cabala Scrinia Ceciliana (1663).

A Collection of Scarce and Valuable Tracts...of the Late Lord Somers, 2nd edn, ed. Walter Scott, vol. 1 (1809).

Digges, Dudley (ed.), *The Compleat Ambassador* (1655).

Forbes, Patrick (ed.), *A Full View of the Public Transactions in the Reign of Queen Elizabeth*, 2 vols (1740).

Haynes, Samuel and Murdin, William (eds), *Collection of State Papers.... Left by William Cecil, Lord Burghley*, 2 vols (1740–59).

Historical Manuscripts Commission 9, *Salisbury*, vols 1–4, 13–14.

de Lettenhove, Kervyn (ed.), *Relations Politiques des Pays-Bas et L'Angleterre...*, 11 vols (Brussels, 1888–1900).

Lodge, E. (ed.), *Illustrations of British History*, 3 vols (1838).

Mackie, R. L. (ed.) *The Letters of James IV, 1505–1513*, Scottish History Society, 3rd Series 45 (1953).

Pollard, A. F. (ed.), *An English Garner: Tudor Tracts, 1532–1588* (New York, 1964).

Wood, Marguerite (ed.), *Flodden Papers: Diplomatic Correspondence between the Courts of France and Scotland*, Scottish History Society, 3rd Series 20 (1933).

Wright, T. (ed.), *Queen Elizabeth and Her Times*, 2 vols (1838).

General Works which Cover All or Part of the Century

Andrew, Kenneth R., *Trade, Plunder and Settlement: Maritime Enterprise and the Genesis of the British Empire, 1480–1630* (Cambridge, 1984).

Crowson, P. S., *Tudor Foreign Policy* (1973).

Doran, Susan, *England and Europe, 1485–1603* (1996).

Guy, John, *Tudor England* (Oxford, 1988).

Loades, David M., *The Reign of Mary I: Politics, Government and Religion in England, 1553–58* (1979, 1991).

MacCaffrey, Wallace T., *The Shaping of the Elizabethan Regime* (1969).

MacCaffrey, Wallace T., *Queen Elizabeth and the Making of Policy, 1572–1588* (Princeton, NJ, 1981).

MacCaffrey, Wallace T., *Elizabeth I: War and Politics, 1588–1603* (New Jersey, 1992).

Potter, David, 'Foreign Policy', in *The Reign of Henry VIII: Politics, Policy and Piety*, ed. Diarmaid MacCulloch (1995).

Quinn, D. B. and Ryan, A. N., *England's Sea Empire, 1550–1642* (1983).

Ramsey, G., 'The Foreign Policy of Elizabeth I', in *The Reign of Elizabeth I*, ed. Christopher Haigh (1984).

Wernham, R. B., *Before the Armada: The Emergence of the English Nation, 1485–1588* (1966).

Wernham, R. B., *The Making of Elizabethan Foreign Policy, 1558–1603* (Berkeley, CA, 1980).

Wernham, R. B., *After the Armada: Elizabethan England and the Struggle for Western Europe, 1588–9* (Oxford, 1984).

Wernham, R. B., *The Return of the Armadas: The Last Years of the Elizabethan War against Spain, 1595–1603* (Oxford, 1994).

Williams, Penry, *The Later Tudors 1485–1603* (Oxford, 1995).

Biographies and Studies of Individuals

Chambers, D. S., 'Cardinal Wolsey and the Papal Tiara', *Bulletin of the Institute of Historical Research*, 38 (1965), pp. 20–30.

Gammon, Samuel Rhea, *Statesman and Schemer: William, First Lord Paget, Tudor Minister* (Newton Abbot, 1973).

Gwyn, Peter, *The King's Cardinal: The Rise and Fall of Thomas Wolsey* (1990).

Hammer, Paul E. J., 'Patronage at Court, Faction and the Earl of Essex' in *The Reign of Elizabeth I: Court and Culture in the Last Decade*, ed. John Guy (1995).

Knecht, R. J., *Francis I* (Cambridge, 1982).

Read, Conyers, *Mr Secretary Walsingham and the Policy of Queen Elizabeth*, 3 vols (Oxford, 1925).

Read, Conyers, *Mr Secretary Cecil and Queen Elizabeth* (London, 1955).

Read, Conyers, *Lord Burghley and Queen Elizabeth* (1960).

Redworth, Glyn, *In Defence of the Catholic Church: The Life of Stephen Gardiner* (Oxford, 1990).

Scarisbrick, J. J., *Henry VIII* (1972).

Thorp, Malcolm, 'William Cecil and the Antichrist: A Study in Anti-Catholic Ideology', in *Politics, Religion and Diplomacy in Early Modern Europe*, ed. Malcolm R. Thorp and Arthur J. Slavin (Kirksville, MO, 1994).

France

Bernard, G., *War Taxation and Rebellion in Early Tudor England: Henry VIII, Wolsey and the Amicable Grant of 1525* (1986).

Davies, C. S. L., 'England and the French War, 1557–59', in *The Mid-Tudor Polity c.1540–1560*, ed. J. Loach and R. Tittler (1980).

Doran, Susan, *Monarchy and Matrimony: The Courtships of Elizabeth I* (1996).

Gunn, Steven, 'The French Wars of Henry VIII', in *The Origins of War in Early-Modern Europe*, ed. J. Black (Edinburgh, 1987).

Gunn, S. J., 'The Duke of Suffolk's March on Paris in 1523', *English Historical Review*, 101 (1986), pp. 596–634.

Harbison, Harris E., *Rival Ambassadors at the Court of Queen Mary* (1940).

Holt, Mack P., *The Duke of Anjou and the Politique Struggle during the Wars of Religion* (Cambridge, 1986).

MacCaffrey, Wallace T., 'The Newhaven Expedition, 1562–1563', *Historical Journal* (1997) pp. 1–21.

Potter, David, 'The Treaty of Boulogne and European Diplomacy, 1549–50', *Bulletin of the Institute of Historical Research*, 55 (1982).

Potter, David, 'The Duc de Guise and the Fall of Calais, 1557–58', *English Historical Review*, 98 (1983) pp. 481–512.
Sutherland, N. M., *The Massacre of Saint Bartholomew and the European Conflict, 1559–1572* (Basingstoke, 1973).

Spain

Adams, Simon, *The Armada Campaign of 1588*, New Appreciations in History 13 (1988).
Andrews, K. R., *Elizabethan Privateering: English Privateering during the Spanish War, 1585–1603* (Cambridge, 1964).
Fernandez-Armesto, Felipe, *The Spanish Armada: The Experience of War in 1588* (Oxford, 1988).
Martin, C. and Parker, G., *The Spanish Armada* (1988).
Rodriguez-Salgado, M. J., *The Changing Face of Empire: Charles V, Philip II and Habsburg Authority, 1551–1559* (Cambridge, 1988).
Rodriguez-Salgado, M. J. and Adams, Simon (eds), *England, Spain and the Gran Armada, 1585–1604* (Edinburgh, 1991).

The Netherlands

Baumann, Wolf-Rüdiger, *The Merchant Adventurers and the Continental Cloth Trade* (Berlin, 1990).
Bisson, Douglas R., *The Merchant Adventurers of England: The Company and the Crown 1474–1564* (Newark, 1993).
Gunn, S. J., 'Wolsey's Foreign Policy and the Domestic Crisis of 1527–8', in *Cardinal Wolsey, Church, State and Art*, ed. S. J. Gunn and P. Lindley (Cambridge, 1991).
Ramsey, G. D., *The City of London in International Politics at the Accession of Elizabeth Tudor* (Manchester, 1975).
Ramsey, G. D., *The Queen's Merchants and the Revolt of the Netherlands: The End of the Antwerp Mart* (Manchester, 1986).
Sutherland, N., 'The Foreign Policy of Queen Elizabeth, the Sea Beggars and the Capture of Brill, 1572', in *Princes, Politics and Religion, 1547–1589* (1984).
Wilson, C., *Queen Elizabeth and the Revolt of the Netherlands* (1970).

Germany and the Baltic

Engelbrecht, Jörg, 'Anglo-German Relations in the Reign of Henry VIII', in *Henry VIII in History, Historiography and Literature*, ed. Uwe Baumann (Frankfurt, 1992).
Lloyd, T. H., *England and the German Hanse, 1157–1611: A Study of their Trade and Commercial Diplomacy* (Cambridge, 1991).
Kouri, E. I., *England and the Attempts to Form a Protestant Alliance in the Late 1560s: A Case-study in European Diplomacy* (Helsinki, 1981).

Kouri, E. I., 'For True Faith or National Interests? Queen Elizabeth and the Protestant Powers', in *Politics and Society in Reformation Europe*, ed. E. I. Kouri and Tom Scott (1989).

McEntergart, Rory, 'Henry VIII and the Marriage to Anne of Cleves', in *Henry VIII: A European Court in England*, ed. David Starkey (1991).

Ramsey, G. D., 'The Settlement of the Merchant Adventurers at Stade, 1587–1611', in *Politics and Society in Reformation Europe*, ed. E. I. Kouri and Tom Scott (1989).

Serawlook Tjernagel, Neelak, *Henry VIII and the Lutherans: A Study in Anglo-Lutheran Relations from 1521 to 1547* (St Louis, MO, 1965).

Willan, T. S., *The Early History of the Russia Company, 1553–1603* (Manchester, 1956).

Zins, Henryk, *England and the Baltic in the Elizabethan Era* (Manchester, 1972).

Scotland

Bonner, Elizabeth, 'The Recovery of St Andrews Castle in 1547: French Naval Policy and Diplomacy in the British Isles', *English Historical Review*, 111 (1996), pp. 578–98.

Bush, M., *The Government Policy of Protector Somerset* (1975).

Dawson, Jane E. A., 'Mary Queen of Scots, Lord Darnley, and Anglo-Scottish Relations in 1565', *The International History Review*, 8 (1986), pp. 4–24.

Dawson, Jane A., 'William Cecil and the British Dimension of Early Elizabethan Foreign Policy', *History*, 74 (1989), pp. 196–216.

Dawson, Jane, 'Anglo-Scottish Protestant Culture and Integration in Sixteenth-Century Britain', in *Conquest and Union: Fashioning a British State, 1485–1725*, ed. Steven G. Ellis and Sarah Barber (Harlow, 1995).

Dunlop, David, 'The Politics of Peace-Keeping: Anglo-Scottish Relations from 1503 to 1511', *Renaissance Studies*, 8 (1994) pp. 138–61.

Head, David M., 'Henry VIII's Scottish Policy', *The Scottish Historical Review*, 61 (1982), pp. 1–24.

Lynch Michael, (ed.), *Mary Stewart, Queen in Three Kingdoms* (Oxford, 1988).

MacDougall, Norman, *James IV* (Edinburgh, 1989).

MacDougall, Norman (ed.), *Scotland and War A.D. 79–1918* (1991).

Mason, Roger A. (ed.), *Scotland and England, 1286–1815* (Edinburgh, 1987).

Mason, Roger A. (ed.), *Scots and Britons: Scottish Political Thought and the Union of 1603* (Cambridge, 1994).

Merriman, Marcus, 'The Assured Scots', *The Scottish Historical Review*, 47 (1968), pp. 10–34.

Merriman, Marcus, 'War and Propaganda during the Rough Wooing', *The Scottish Tradition*, 9–10 (1979–80), pp. 20–30.

Merriman, Marcus, 'The High Road from Scotland: Stewarts and the Tudors in the Mid-sixteenth Century', in *Uniting the Kingdom? The Making of British History*, ed. Alexander Grant and Keith J. Stringer (1995).

Morgan, Hiram, 'British Policies before the British Isles', in *The British Problem c.1534–1707: State Formation in the Atlantic Archipelago*, ed. Brendan Bradshaw and John Morrill (1996).

Rae, Thomas I., *The Administration of the Scottish Frontier, 1513–1603* (Edinburgh, 1966).
Wormold, Jenny, *Mary Queen of Scots: A Study in Failure* (1991).

Ireland

Morgan, Hiram, *Tyrone's Rebellion: The Outbreak of the Nine Years War in Tudor Ireland* (Woodbridge, 1993).
Palmer, William, *The Problem of Ireland in Tudor Foreign Policy, 1485–1603* (Woodbridge, 1994).
Potter, David, 'French Intrigue in Ireland during the Reign of Henri II, 1547–1559', *The International History Review*, 5 (1983), pp. 159–180.
Silke, John J., *Kinsale* (Liverpool, 1970).

The Papacy

Bayne, C. G., *Anglo-Roman Relations, 1558–1565* (Oxford, 1913).
Lutz, Heinrich, 'Cardinal Reginald Pole and the Path to Anglo-Papal Mediation at the Peace Conference of Marq, 1553–55', in *Politics and Society in Reformation Europe*, ed. E. I. Kouri and Tom Scott (1987).
MacGrath, Patrick, *Papists and Puritans under Elizabeth I* (1967).
Parmiter, G. de C., *The King's Great Matter: A Study of Anglo-Papal Relations, 1527–34* (1967).
Wilkie, W. E., *The Cardinal Protectors of England: Rome and the Tudors before the Reformation* (Cambridge, 1974).

Unpublished Dissertations

Adams, S., 'The Protestant Cause: Religious Alliance with the European Calvinist Communities as a Political Issue in England 1585–1630', DPhil, University of Oxford (1973).
Favereau, Julio Retamal, 'Anglo-Spanish Relations 1566–72: The Mission of Don Guerau de Spes at London, with a Preliminary Consideration of that of Mr John Man at Madrid', DPhil, University of Oxford (1972).
Leiman, Mitchell, 'Sir Francis Walsingham and the Anjou Marriage Plan, 1574–81', PhD, University of Cambridge (1989).
Lock, Julian, 'Strange Usurped Potentates: Elizabeth I, the Papacy and the Indian Summer of the Medieval Deposing Power', DPhil, University of Oxford (1992).
MacMahon, L., 'The English Invasion of France 1544', MA, University of Warwick (1992).
McEntegart, Rory, 'England and the League of Schmalkaden 1531–47: Faction, Foreign Policy and the English Reformation', PhD, University of London (1992).

Potter, D. L., 'Diplomacy in the Mid 16th Century: England and France 1536–1550', PhD, University of Cambridge (1973).

Richardson, Glenn, 'Anglo-French Political and Cultural Relations during the Reign of Henry VIII', PhD, University of London (1995).

INDEX

141